12/03

D0013781

Customs
and
Etiquette

Saudi

Customs and

Etiquette

KATHY CUDDIHY

STACEY INTERNATIONAL

Saudi Customs and Etiquette

published by
Stacey International
128 Kensington Church Street
London W8 4BH
Tel: +44 (0) 207 221 7166
Fax:+44 (0) 207 792 9288
E-mail: enquiries@stacey-international.co.uk
Website: www.stacey-international.co uk

© **Kathy Cuddihy 2002**

All rights reserved. No part of this publication may be
reproduced, stored in a retrieval system or transmitted
in any form or by any means, electronic, mechanical,
photographic or otherwise, without prior permission
of the copyright owner.

ISBN: 1 900988 52 6

British Library Cataloguing-in-Publication Data
A catalogue record for this publication
is available from the British Library

Design & drawings by
Kitty Carruthers & Sam Crooks

Printed & bound by
Oriental Press, Dubai

390
, 09538
CUD
2002

ACKNOWLEDGEMENTS

I have been blessed in my many Saudi friends, each one of whom is part of the rich tapestry of my experiences in Saudi Arabia. In one way or another, all of them have contributed to the information contained in this book.

Every attempt has been made accurately to transfer their cultural awareness to these pages. The responsibility for any possible misinterpretation is solely the author's.

CONTENTS

CONTENTS (CONT.)

AUTHOR'S PREFACE

I knew virtually nothing about Saudi Arabia when I came to Riyadh in 1976. Few Westerners did. For the most part, written information was limited; hearsay tended to be negative and, too often, inaccurate.

Unfortunately, the situation is little changed today. Publication of books on Kingdom-related topics has increased significantly but foreigners continue to arrive woefully unprepared for the sometimes dramatic adaptations required of them.

Because of linguistic, religious and cultural barriers, successful integration into Saudi society does not come easily. I can only stress that knowing and understanding the Saudi people is a rewarding experience and worth the effort required to make those first advances.

Saudi Customs and Etiquette attempts to bridge the culture gap. The book does not pretend to be a comprehensive guide to Saudi Arabia's rich heritage. Instead, I have limited my choice of topics to those which particularly interest or affect foreigners. The information has been kept short and concise for purposes of easy reference and quick assimilation.

I hope this book will allow readers to breach the real or imagined boundaries which exist between cultures and will instil a confidence to venture beyond the isolation of expatriate compounds.

An assignment in Saudi Arabia is an opportunity to broaden cultural horizons. Take advantage of the experience! A positive attitude will ensure that your encounters will enrich you.

Kathy Cuddihy
Riyadh, August 2002

CHAPTER ONE
HOSPITALITY

NE OF THE first things that impresses visitors to Saudi Arabia is the welcoming attitude of their Saudi hosts. It soon becomes obvious that hospitality in the fullest sense of the word is an inherent feature of Saudi tradition.

The predominantly nomadic lifestyle of previous generations made the custom one of necessity in a fight for survival: a person in the position to offer hospitality today might be in dire need of it himself tomorrow. Refusal of food and shelter could mean death in Arabia's harsh environment. Since no one was immune to the possibility of requiring unexpected assistance from friend or foe, the practice of hospitality became a refined art. Even an enemy entering an encampment in peace could remain as a privileged guest for three days before being asked his name or the purpose of his journey. The 'bond of salt' put the guest under the protection of the host, not just for the time of his visit but for three days after his departure.

The expression *When you offer hospitality, pour riches* reflects an ingrained code of conduct designed to ensure a guest's pleasure, although it could mean deprivation for the family. The honour of generosity is an important facet of the Arab personality. Even in modern urban society an almost sacred observance of the unwritten rules of hospitality persists.

Greetings

As-salaam alaikum (peace be with you) is a universal salutation among Arabs. The standard reply, *Wa alaikum as-salaam,* means 'and upon you, peace'. *Ahlan wasahlan,* another frequent form of address, means 'welcome'. *Ahlan feek,* the response, translates as 'welcome to you'. Visitors who learn these basic greetings show a courtesy which will be much appreciated by Saudi hosts. If you can't master the Arabic phrases, always remember to extend a friendly greeting in English or your own language. Arabs appreciate this courtesy as basic good manners.

In addition to a structured series of verbal exchanges, Saudis greet each other with kisses. Because these displays can differ from region to region, foreigners usually find it fascinating to watch the ritual but confusing to be directly involved. To avoid embarassment, Saudis simply shake hands with foreigners unless they have become close friends.

The greeting kiss generally falls into one of the following categories: nose, forehead, right shoulder, hand, or right and left cheeks. Elderly people receive a final kiss on the forehead. Established friends and family members kiss on the right cheek and then two or three times on the left cheek. Cheek kissing actually resembles hugging since the lips do not touch the face. This relatively recent tradition arrived from Mediterranean countries within the last century. Only offspring or those regarded as offspring kiss on the hands to show special respect. The nose is considered the noblest feature, so a kiss there denotes the highest esteem. Kissing on the right shoulder is reserved for the king or princes but a handshake is replacing this practice.

Saudi men and women don't traditionally shake hands with each other but they often make exceptions where foreigners are concerned. Typically, they shake hands by locking thumbs and holding the fingers straight out. The result is an almost stationary clasp rather than a vigorous grip. A Western man meeting an Arab woman should allow her to make the first move to shake hands. She may prefer to refrain from this gesture of personal contact. By the same token, some Muslim men may refuse to shake a woman's hand. Usually, even liberal Saudis will avoid this contact immediately before prayer.

Prescribed small talk follows the welcome gestures and is expected both in business and socially. Foreigners who do not indulge in this custom may appear impatient or rude to Saudis. Enquiries should be made about the health and well-being of the individual and his or her family. In prolonged, purely social conversations, it is discourteous to introduce unpleasant topics.

Don't use ritual expressions such as "Let's get together for lunch" unless you mean what you say. If you haven't acted on your comment within a reasonable period of time, you risk compromising your sincerity in the eyes of Arab friends or colleagues.

Respect for Elders

Saudis traditionally show great respect for their elders. In most encounters, age usually takes precedence, even over status. The eldest person is accorded the first greeting. If socializing extends beyond greetings, he or she is given the most prominent seating position and receives food and beverage before the other guests. The exception to the rule can occur when a high-ranking member of the royal family is present. Depending on the circumstances and the formality of the occasion, the prince or princess may nevertheless defer to age.

The Coffee Ritual

Although wild coffee plants originated in Ethiopia (Kaffa), it was in Arabia where they were first cultivated in the 15th century. One legend attributes the discovery of coffee to Kaldi, an Arab goat-herd who, in AD 850, noticed the friskiness of his goats after they ate the red berries. It is not known when or why he progressed from chewing the berries to roasting and brewing them, but his breakthrough had great impact on future generations. The full-bodied *Arabica* bean accounts for two-thirds of world coffee consumption.

In Arabia, nothing symbolizes the tradition of hospitality more than the ritual serving of coffee, a gesture which conveys cordiality and welcome. The preparation of coffee has remained virtually unchanged throughout the centuries. Even in modern offices and many urban homes, where the method has been modified to meet the requirements of a faster-paced lifestyle with an emphasis on convenience, the ceremony survives recognizably intact.

In the most traditional settings, green beans are lightly roasted over a fire in a long-handled, ladle-like utensil called a *mahmasa*. In order not to let the beans become too dark, the *mahmasa* is gently turned and kept away from the flame. The roasting beans are stirred with an equally long-handled implement (*yad al-mahmasa*) with a broad, flat end. When the beans begin to glow, they are placed in a wooden coffee box or tray (*mubarrad*) about 15-20 centimetres long and with a partially-covered funnel opening at the narrower end.

The cooled beans are then coarsely and rhythmically ground in a mortar, or *nijr*, made from wood, stone, or brass. The ringing music from the *nijr* invites anyone within earshot to come for coffee. Each tribe has its own *nijr* rhythm that distinguishes it from the sounds made by other tribes.

Water is placed in a *dallah*. With its rounded lower half and its pelican-beak spout, this distinctive coffee pot has become a symbol of Saudi hospitality. The ground coffee is added and brought to the boil. The vital ingredient of cardamom, and perhaps saffron and other spices to give extra flavour and colour, is added to the brew which is then brought to the boil once again. Either crushed or in pods, cardamom gives the brew a taste unique to this part of the world. Taken before a meal, cardamom prepares the stomach lining to accept food; after a meal, it aids digestion.

The steaming, aromatic liquid is poured from the *dallah* in a long, thin jet. A sprig of dried palm webbing (*leefah*) placed in the spout is an ancient method of filtration which prevents the grounds and spices from entering the cups.

The yellowish coffee is drunk without sugar or milk from small bowl-shaped cups without handles. In order to keep the coffee hot, the cups are only a third or half filled. The server will replenish the coffee as often as necessary but guests should accept no more than three cups unless socializing with close friends. While there is no obligation to drink the coffee, it is courteous to accept one cup as an acknowledgement of the host's hospitality.

To indicate that he does not want more coffee, the guest wobbles the cup from side to side or, in some areas, covers the cup with the palm of the hand before returning it to the server. Guests should accept and return cups with their right hand.

In traditional homes, fresh dates often accompany Arabic coffee. These delicious fruits bear little resemblance to the dried varieties found in export markets. So far, more than 400 commercial classifications of dates have been recorded in the Kingdom. Experts distinguish types by shape (oval or round, large or small), colour (reddish, or bright or dark yellow), and taste. Connoisseurs liken the taste and texture of top-grade dates to truffle chocolates; lesser grades have a comparatively tough consistency, rather like soft toffee. An old adage proclaims, *If you are hungry and eat dates, you will be full. If you are full and eat dates, it will be easy to digest.*

The most popular stage of the date's development is called *rutab*: the partially ripened date is half brown and half yellow or red and has a pleasant combination of rough and smooth textures. Dates which have fully ripened and turned completely brown are called *tamr*. Fresh dates can be stored in the freezer but should not be kept in the refrigerator.

Sweet tea customarily appears after the Arabic coffee and dates. It is sipped from small, handled glasses in roughly triple the quantity of the coffee. Sometimes, instead of regular tea, infusions such as *nanaa* (fresh mint), *karkaday* (hibiscus flowers), or *yansoon* (aniseed) are served. These are medicinal as well as refreshing: *nanaa* helps digestion and fights nausea; *karkaday* fights colds and stabilizes blood pressure; *yansoon* soothes coughs. It is also effective against indigestion and as a remedy to treat flatulence and colic. After tea, coffee is served once again.

Invitations

Foreigners should feel especially honoured if a Saudi invites them to his home to share a meal. In the case of a spontaneous invitation, it is appropriate to refuse politely once or twice before accepting graciously. If possible, written invitations should be replied to in the language in which they are received.

In most situations, punctuality is expected, especially at small, private gatherings. Nevertheless, Arab guests tend to arrive at Western homes later than other guests. This is partly because Westerners usually entertain much earlier than Arabs and partly because Saudi office hours often extend to early evening. Dinner invitations around 8:30 p.m. make it easier for Arab guests to be on time. At large receptions, such as a wedding party, some guests arrive up to two or three hours late. Westerners who arrive punctually at these events usually don't have much company for the first hour or so.

When strangers come to the home, many Arab families prefer to have the men eat apart from the women. Sometimes only men will be invited to dinner. Foreign couples should not assume that both of them are included in an invitation. A tactful confirmation beforehand saves potential embarrassment for everyone.

Saudi men and women normally socialize separately in public. Foreigners who invite Saudi couples should not be surprised if only the husband arrives, despite the fact that he may have accepted the invitation for his wife as well. A Saudi gentleman would prefer to make polite excuses for his wife's absence rather than explain cultural differences or possibly cause offense by refusing the invitation altogether. In place of the wife he may bring one or two friends—without notifying the hostess in advance. At typically large Saudi gatherings where there is always a surplus of food this presents no problem. The unexpected arrivals might not be so easy to accommodate at a sitdown dinner for eight!

When inviting more than one Saudi to a private gathering, foreigners should discreetly ensure that each feels comfortable with the other(s) in a social situation.

Saudis often won't give much advance warning when extending a social invitation. Likewise, they prefer not to have to make a commitment too far ahead. It is perfectly acceptable to invite a Saudi friend only a couple of days before an event. Be prepared, especially at larger functions, that a Saudi who may already have confirmed attendance may not show up. It's entirely likely that the hostess won't receive advance warning of the change in plans.

Eating

Many Saudi families, particularly those in cities, have adopted the Western custom of eating at a table but in traditional households the platters of food are still served on a circular mat (*sufra*) or on a rectangular plastic cover spread on the floor. Family and friends sit cross-legged around the perimeter of the display and use their right hands to serve themselves. Foreign guests unaccustomed to the Saudi method of eating with fingers are usually offered a spoon. Nevertheless, it is courteous to try to comply with local custom.

Eating begins after carefully washing the hands and uttering the phrase *Bismillah ar-rahman ar-rahim*, meaning 'In the name of God, the most gracious, the most merciful.' Food is handled with the right hand only. When eating from a communal dish, the fingers should never touch the mouth or tongue. Each person should confine himself to his own 'wedge' of food and draw food towards himself. To show respect and to make sure that no one goes hungry, participants pass the choicest morsels to a guest or to another eating companion. It is impolite to refuse such offerings or to refrain from making similar gestures.

An Arab host takes pride in providing copious quantities of food. He would fail in his social obligations if he allowed anyone to leave his table hungry. Even in times when food was less plentiful, a host would encourage the guest to eat to his satisfaction and would never reveal the extent of his own hunger. Saudi hosts will repeatedly encourage their guests to eat. Western guests who pace themselves accordingly can have two or three helpings,

SIMMS LIBRARY ALBUQUERQUE ACADEMY

thereby satisfying their hosts and themselves. Leaving some food on the plate assures the host that a guest has eaten sufficiently.

Saudis participate in pleasant, prolonged conversation beforehand but the act of eating is taken fairly seriously. At traditional meals, little social talk takes place.

After a meal, participants offer the thanksgiving *Ilhamdullilah* (thanks be to God) and wash their hands and mouths. At large gatherings, guests may leave when they finish eating. Other guests should not feel that they have to finish at the same time. A host will often linger to show his appreciation of the guests' company. *An'am allah alaikum kather allah kherkum* conveys the wish that Allah be generous to the host or hostess and lets him/her know that the meal was enjoyed. Unlike the Western practice of lingering after dinner, guests in a Saudi home should leave shortly after eating or immediately after the presentation of incense at formal gatherings.

Until recently, foreigners seldom experienced authentic Saudi cuisine unless they had the rare opportunity to visit a Saudi home or attend a wedding. Now, thanks to increasingly popular Saudi-themed restaurants, this culinary heritage is being shared with and appreciated by a wider audience. Many of the traditional recipes are quite different from the Lebanese fare that passes as the standard for Arabic cuisine.

Smoking

Although health awareness programmes are beginning to erode the deep-rooted habit of cigarette smoking, the attraction of the ancient water pipe is increasing in popularity. This tall, elegant, smoking apparatus is known locally as a 'hubbly-bubbly' because of the sound the water makes as it filters into a water-filled base. It is also referred to as a *shisha* or *narghile* in Arabic, meaning 'coconut'. In former times, the cooling water was kept in a coconut shell.

The tobacco mixture, flavoured with fruit or a herb and honey blend, sits in a clay bowl at the top of the *shisha* (pronounced 'sheesha', from the Persian for the glass water-holder) and is covered in glowing charcoal embers. A glass bowl contains the water which cools the smoke. Two tubes extend from the glass bowl: a rigid one leading to the pipe bowl that holds the tobacco and a long, flexible one tipped with a filter/nozzle from which the smoker tranquilly inhales.

The *shisha* is decidedly less portable than a pack of cigarettes; *shisha* smokers therefore tend to gather at cafés dedicated to this socially amenable activity and spend several hours at a time puffing contentedly. These public cafés are exclusively for men but it is acceptable for women to smoke the *shisha* in private.

Although *shisha* smoking is not associated with cancer, the long, deep breaths required to smoke the pipe can cause emphysema. Users should be aware that germs come not just from the nozzles (most regulars have their own nozzles and cafés provide clean nozzles for customers) but from the tubes themselves which cannot be disinfected. Only if the *shisha* is used exclusively by the same person can the risk of respiratory infections be prevented.

Mint Tea

Ingredients

1 litre of boiling water
1 to 2 cups of fresh mint leaves
1 to 2 tablespoons of green tea leaves*
sugar to taste

Method

Steep the ingredients in a teapot for about five minutes. Serve in special tea glasses with a fresh sprig of mint in each. Sweeten to taste.

For variation, replace the mint with fresh orange blossoms, a few drops of orange blossom water, or a large pinch of dried orange peel.

*Regular tea (loose or in bags) may be used. Alternatively, eliminate the tea leaves and use only mint.

Arabic Coffee

Ingredients
1 Arabic coffee cup of lightly browned coffee beans
1 Arabic coffee cup of cardamom *(hail)*

Method
Coarsely grind the coffee beans. Fill a Saudi-style coffee pot* 3/4 full with water. Heat the water until it boils. Add the ground coffee. Gently bring the mixture to the boil. Remove the pot from the heat and strain the liquid. Pour the filtered coffee into a second Saudi-style coffee pot and add the cardamom. For a more subtle flavour, use whole cardamom. Increase or decrease the quantity according to taste. Place the pot on low heat. Serve just before the coffee begins to boil. Palm webbing—or modern plastic imitation substitute—placed at the spout prevents the grounds from being poured into the cups.

As a sign of respect, always serve the most senior guests first. If all the guests are of approximately the same age, serve the coffee from the right side and continue around the room to the left. Hold the pot with the left hand and the cups in a stack in the right hand. Excess cups can be placed in an inverted stack on the left thumb. Pour one cup at a time, letting each guest take his or her own cup. Put used cups at the bottom of the stack.

*Any pot can be used, but the Saudi-style *qahwa* pot (*dallah*) adds ambiance to the procedure.

Ginger Infusion

This is a popular drink in the winter. The spicy ginger gives a pleasant warming sensation as it is swallowed.

Ingredients
2 tablespoons ground ginger
boiling water
a pinch of saffron
sugar or honey to taste

Method
Add ginger and saffron to boiling water and cool slightly. Pour the hot liquid from one pot to another to minimize sediment. The infusion can be taken without sweeteners but it is common to add sugar or honey to taste.

CHAPTER TWO

INCENSE

SINCE CIVILIZATION BEGAN, humans have been attracted to the properties of incense. Records show that a lucrative frankincense trade agreement existed between King Solomon and the Queen of Sheba (*Sa'ba*). The Roman historian Pliny discloses that Nero burned more than the equivalent of Arabia's entire annual frankincense production—over 6,000 tons—at the funeral of his wife Poppea. Ancient Egyptian art portrays Pharaohs swinging censers. Ovid and Virgil made reference to incense in their great classical writings.

In ancient Arabia, gum-resins produced by trees of the genera *Boswellia sacra* and *Commiphora* provided the primary sources of frankincense and myrrh (from the Arabic word *murrah*, meaning 'bitter').

Incisions made in the trunks cause a fluid to ooze from the bark's resin ducts. Upon exposure to the air, the irregularly-shaped, gummy globules slowly harden over a period of two to three weeks and are then ready for harvesting. Each tree can be tapped up to four times in the four-month season. Cracking open the lumps, or 'tears,' reveals semi-opaque colours which range from the almost transparent white or blue-green tinges of the purest varieties to yellow-brown or reddish hues of lesser value. The resins have little or no aroma until they have been exposed to heat which brings out a balsamic odor.

Boswellia sacra yields the best quality frankincense. Indigenous to the Dhofar region of Oman, this resource brought the area immense wealth approximately 3,000 years ago. By AD 100, local sovereigns had secured a monopoly of Arabian incense, increasing both their economic and political advantages.

From the well-protected harbour of Sumhuram, in southern Oman, ships sailed to all parts of the known world with their precious cargoes. Overland routes along the west side of Arabia saw lengthy camel caravans threading their way to destinations as far away as India and Rome. The punishment for traders who deviated from the established itinerary was death. This ensured that regional rulers could collect the heavy taxes they imposed on this valuable commodity.

Incense originally gained prominence in religious rituals. It established the presence of deities (fragrance being a divine characteristic) and gratified them. Early civilizations considered the perfumed scent one of the most venerable offerings to gods and believed that the high-rising smoke symbolized ascending prayers.

Incense also had many secular applications. The aromatic aspect of the smoke served as a fumigant in areas of poor sanitation and in times of plague. It is still burned in the evenings to repel insects. It also alleviates the lassitude caused by Arabia's heat and humidity.

As a pharmacological and veterinary ingredient, the gum-resin reputedly cured a variety of ills, from simple bruises to more complicated ailments such as dysentery and kidney disorders. Pliny the Elder mentioned frankincense as an antidote to hemlock poisoning. Even today, some people add a few lumps of incense to water to purify it for drinking purposes.

Modern medicine has not found any scientific basis to validate the more dramatic traditional remedies. Nevertheless, there are indications of its effectiveness in the treatment of digestive disorders and skin ailments. Myrrh, particularly, has slight antiseptic, astringent, and curative properties.

Non-medicinal uses of incense included cosmetic applications, such as depilatories, deodorants, fixatives in perfumes, and as a sealant for teeth. As a volatile oil, incense reputedly retards aging of the skin. If proven accurate, this factor alone could cause a frenzied revival of the incense trade!

Wealthy people used the more expensive myrrh as a sacred anointing oil and embalming fluid, as well as for cooking and fumigation.

Due to a gradual decrease in demand, frankincense and myrrh production levels have dropped substantially. Today, most people in Saudi Arabia burn scented woods such as sandalwood. In Arabic, these woods are collectively referred to as *'ood*.

'Ood is generally less expensive than frankincense or myrrh, but high quality woods can be extravagantly priced. The best *'ood* originates in India; however, due to almost exhausted supplies, the Indian government now prohibits its export. Currently, *'ood* comes from Burma, Cambodia,

Malaysia and Indonesia, in descending order of quality.

'Ood is weighed by a denomination called *al wagiya*, which equals 31.1 grams (one troy ounce). Top grade *'ood* can cost more than SR3,000 per *wagiya*.

Ma'amoul is another popular form of incense in Saudi Arabia. These round, dark balls consist of lower grade powdered *'ood* blended with rose water or, more rarely, sandalwood oil, to form a dough-like substance. The quality of the ingredients determines the cost of the *ma'amoul*. After two days, the mixture is cut into small pieces. The moisture is squeezed from each one and the balls sit on a tray to dry further.

Incense Burners

A traditional incense burner or censer is called a *medkhana*. *Medkhanas* are crafted from a number of materials, including unbaked clay, wood, stone, or metals. The basic shape of the *medkhana* has remained unchanged for more than 2,000 years: a square base mounted by four legs supports a square receptacle for small pieces of incense which are placed on several lumps of glowing charcoal.

Contemporary Saudis usually choose imported models made from metals such as aluminium, brass, silver, or gold. In Saudi Arabia, only in Hail, a city 700 kilometers north of Riyadh, do *medkhanas* continue to be made in the traditional manner. Using hand-forged tools, local craftsmen fashion censers from solid blocks of tamarisk (*athl*) wood, a process which takes an average of six days from start to finish. Decorative touches can include bronze studs, brass sheeting with geometric designs, and small mirrors embedded in the sides, a throwback to primitive superstitions which held that reflective objects repel evil spirits.

Incense represents expressions of both welcome and farewell and is a salient segment of important ceremonies or the recognition of special guests. When the gently smoking *medkhana* is passed, each person fans the redolent wisps of smoke into the hair and clothing, where the pleasant aroma can linger for several days. A lovely Arabic saying expresses the wish, *Incense so you will return.*

CHAPTER THREE

HEALTH & BEAUTY

RABS HAVE A long history of high standards in personal hygiene.The Crusaders adopted the habit of public baths and carried the concept with them from the Middle East back to Europe. To emphasize the importance attached to cleanliness, the holy *Quran* makes ritual cleansing (*wudho'a*) a requirement before each of the five daily prayers.

Traditional Oral Hygiene

Saudi fastidiousness in matters of cleanliness includes oral hygiene. Since the time of the Babylonians (5000 BC), Arabs relied on the *miswak* to clean their teeth, freshen their breath, prevent plaque build-up and stimulate the gums. Today, toothbrushes prevail but the *miswak* remains a popular supplement to oral hygiene. Scientific studies confirm the benefits: sinnegrin, tannic acid and sodium carbonate in the root act as natural antiseptics. Some of the other properties include anti-inflammatory substances, fluoride, and silicone which helps clean the teeth.

In Saudi Arabia, the slightly bitter tasting *miswak* comes from the root of the arak tree (*salvadora persica*). After soaking the *miswak* in water for several hours, one or two layers of the bark are pared off one end of 20 cm-long stick-like pieces to form bristles. Briefly chewing the exposed fibers softens the *miswak* sufficiently for brushing.

The *miswak* is used much like a regular toothbrush. First massage the gums with the bristles and then apply downward strokes on the upper teeth and upward strokes on the lower teeth, brushing both inner and outer surfaces. Remove worn fibres and expose new ones by further paring.

The *miswak* is commonly used during the holy month of Ramadan to freshen the mouth. Brushing with a regular toothbrush during the day is not recommended because of the risk of swallowing water.

Traditional Health Care

Before the advent of clinics and hospitals throughout the Kingdom, Saudis relied on herbal medicine, food cures, and/or cauterization. Although cauterization usually did more harm than good, other methods of treatment were effective, particularly for skin, stomach and urinary tract infections. Fortunately, a restricted but healthy diet and a physically active lifestyle gave most people a hardy constitution.

In addition to a variety of medicinal herbs and shrubs, the most common ingredients used to treat ailments were myrrh, aniseed, henna, black caraway, fenugreek, ground coffee beans and tar oil. Toxic substances were known to relieve inflammation. Fried dates blended with oil were a popular antidote for sprains. Yellow turmeric served as both a make-up and a sunscreen. Tribes living near coastal areas used ground red coral to heal cuts.

Today, despite the prevalence of well-equipped hospitals, many Saudi families continue to rely on traditional cures for common ailments. *Murrah* (myrrh) is the most universal of remedies. This tree resin, found mainly in Yemen, has an antibiotic effect and is particularly good for healing wounds. The lumps of resin are soaked in hot water to form a beverage. *Murrah* can also be applied as an ointment. Pleasant tasting *rashad* is another popular remedy that is good for coughs and mending bones. Equally effective for bone injuries but foul tasting is *helba*, a seed that can be boiled in water or taken as a powder.

Perfume

Association with a good person
is like meeting a perfumer:
even if you don't buy from him,
you come away smelling good.

Exotic fragrances are an integral part of Saudi culture. Saudis — both men and women — generously apply scent to their bodies, including liberal splashes on the hands after washing. The Prophet Mohammed claimed that only perfume gave equal pleasure to both the wearer and the bystander. The second caliph, Umar bin al-Khattab, declared that if he had not been caliph he would have been a perfumer because the beautiful smell would enrich him even if the business lost money.

Of all the scent bases, *dehn al ward*, the essence of crushed rose petals, remains the favourite. In Saudi Arabia the production of perfume occurs only in Taif and its environs. According to local opinion, the wild roses which grow in the nearby Al Hadda mountains make the best concentrate. Each manufacturer steadfastly believes that Taif's ideal climate produces an unrivalled quality of perfume. They will not use other types of flowers, nor will they even use any roses other than those from Taif. This conviction is so strong that the industry operates only 40 days each year, in April/May, when the wild mountain roses bloom. It is the unadulterated nature of Arabian perfume which makes it so popular—and expensive.

Steam distillation produces the essential oils. With correct temperature control, condensation gradually forms in glass jugs which are connected by pipes to vats of rose petals and water.

It takes approximately ten hours to fill a ten-litre jug on the first run. This yields mostly the valuable oil concentrate plus a small amount of rose water. During the second run, in which it takes eight hours to fill ten litres, the yield of rose water far exceeds that of oil concentrate. The third and final run of seven hours produces only low grade rose water.

In Saudi Arabia, rose water is used primarily as a subtle flavouring in cooking and to enhance drinking water. The usual proportions are one or two teaspoons of rose water per two litres of ordinary water, or to taste. Rose water reputedly benefits the heart and stomach.

Good quality rose water can be distinguished from poorer grades by shaking the bottle. With the best water, a density of tiny air bubbles remains suspended for as long as half a minute. Relatively few bubbles appear in lesser grades.

Taste, too, indicates excellence. The best waters have a hot and bitingly bitter flavour before dilution. After a few minutes, however, the concentrated liquid provokes a warming sensation in the chest.

Henna

The small, fragrant henna flower (*faghiya*) comes from the shrub *Lawsonia inermis* which is prevalent in the Middle East and North Africa. Henna is another prevalent perfume ingredient in Arabia. Local *suqs* (markets) also sell the scented oil concentrate, *dehn al faghiya*.

Foreigners associate the henna shrub primarily with the rich natural dye used so frequently in the Middle East. Henna (*hinna'*) can range in tone from pink to orange, red, burnished copper and even black. The addition of other plant leaves, such as indigo, tea, coffee, cloves and lemon, produce shade variations. Body heat influences the colour intensity. The fact that reds and oranges are considered festive, lucky colours no doubt has contributed to much of henna's popularity.

Henna tattoos have become a popular fashion accessory around the world. Users should beware of the black henna that is in common usage in the West. This is natural henna mixed with a black chemical dye called PPD (P-Phenylenediamine). When applied directly to the skin it can cause allergic reactions.

One of henna's most widespread functions is as a hair and scalp treatment: add hot water to pure henna powder until the henna becomes thick and creamy. Apply to the hair immediately, coating each strand, from scalp to tip. Leave for about an hour and then rinse and shampoo as normal.

The colourant strengthens hair and gives it a silken sheen. Because henna does not penetrate the hair shaft, it is harmless if applied correctly. If used too frequently over prolonged periods, however, henna may make hair brittle and produce orange tones. It is not suitable for light-coloured or grey hair.

Henna is also used as a dye and moisturizer for the soles of the feet and the palms and backs of the hands. It is believed to stabilize sensitive skin. When mixed with egg and applied to toenails and fingernails, henna acts as a strengthening agent. Some tribes believe that henna spread over exposed surfaces keeps the body cool in the intense Arabian sun.

Besides proven herbal qualities, henna has decorative appeal. Saudis tend to prefer large floral motifs, although designs might vary according to the occasion, for example grain patterns at harvest time or more intricate flowers for a wedding. Many communities have their own exclusive templates by which they can be identified.

The application of henna in lace-like patterns on the hands and feet is a specialized, time-consuming art. Dried, finely ground henna leaves are mixed with a small amount of water or eucalyptus oil and strained lemon juice to form an elastic consistency. Petrol may be added to speed the process and deepen the colour. After letting the mixture settle for at least one hour but no more than 24 hours, the henna artist paints the moist henna onto the skin in floral or geometric designs with a pointed object, usually a toothpick or needle, or a device like a pastry cone.

For the less artistic, the *suqs* sell ready-made patterns for tracing intricate designs onto the hands. A coating of mustard oil, or a blend of lemon juice, sugar, pepper and garlic gently swabbed onto the painted areas prevents the drying henna from flaking and will help to intensify the colour. The stain can last for as long as four weeks if the painted areas remain undisturbed for approximately five hours after the application. The dye should not become wet for the first 12 hours after having the henna scraped off. During this period the colour becomes stronger.

In many rural areas, particularly among the bedouin, henna application becomes almost ritualistic on the night before a marriage (but only for the woman's first marriage). The female members of the wedding party gather together for the *lailat al hinna'* (night of henna) to have their hands and feet richly adorned. Hiding the groom's name or initials within the detailed pattern can make the wedding night more interesting! The bride wears pretty, embroidered bags over her hands to avoid staining her clothes. She keeps the bags as a wedding memento. Etiquette dictates that none of the guests has more elaborate designs applied than the bride.

Of course, not everyone goes to such trouble, especially for everyday use. Some women simply hold a ball of henna in each hand and wrap their fists tightly in towels at night so they can sleep while the henna takes effect.

Kohl

Just as henna enhances the hands, feet and hair, *kohl* beautifies the eyes.

In Arabic, the word *kohl* refers to any substance that goes on the eyelid or around the eye margin. *Kohl* has been popular for thousands of years in this part of the world, not only as a beauty preparation but also as medication. In former times, it was used to prevent or fight eye infections. Its black, shiny properties were thought to shield the eyes from the glare and reflection of the sun. This probably influenced the belief that *kohl* cleared or improved vision.

The Prophet Mohammed encouraged the use of *kohl* but he specified the variety made from *ethmid*, a stone which consists mainly of antimony trisulphide. This inert substance does not irritate the mucous membranes. Today, *ethmid* is rare and most commercial *kohl* contains up to 88% lead sulphide concentration. It looks similar to *ethmid* but, as a toxic substance, it can cause many problems if introduced into the eye itself. One effect is chronic lead poisoning, particularly in children.

There are currently almost 30 different kinds of *kohl* on the market. Some include organic materials such as camphor or sandalwood. Certain types have proven antibacterial effects but many are heavily contaminated. Only reputable brands are recommended.

An Arab Poet's Description of a Beautiful Woman

Hair black as the feathers of the ostrich
Forehead wide and eyebrows thick and arched
Eyes black like a wild doe
Nose straight and finely modelled
Cheeks like bouquets of roses
Mouth small and round
Teeth like pearls set in coral
Lips small and coloured like vermilion
Neck white and long
Shoulders broad
Hands and feet small
Manners agreeable
Laughter delicate

CHAPTER FOUR

DRESS

HE FIRST THING that strikes foreigners about Saudi dress is the uniformity of men's clothing and the anonymity of women's outer wear. Despite the sometimes extensive changes in lifestyle experienced throughout Saudi Arabia in recent decades, fashions have remained basically unaltered. While some Saudis have converted to Western dress when it is more suitable to the demands of their work environment, most continue to find the traditional designs a satisfactory concession to both harsh climate and religious convention. Retaining this striking feature of their heritage sustains Saudi identity when it might otherwise become diluted in the process of making a rapid transition to modernity. As an integral feature of the Arabian personality, this custom is likely to remain intact for the foreseeable future.

Men

In the 9th century AD, an envoy sent by Emperor Charlemagne presented his credentials at the court of Baghdad's Caliph Haroon Al-Rashid. The envoy removed his plumed hat with a flourish and made a sweeping bow. The act provoked the caliph to enquire if there was anything wrong with the honourable envoy's head. "It's the West's way of expressing respect, Sire," the caliph was told.

"Tell my valued friend," Haroon Al-Rashid relayed to the interpreter, "that here in the East the headgear must stay on the head in order to convey respect."

The white cotton *ghutrah* or the red-and-white checked *sham'agh* head covering serves both as protection from the sun and as a convenient nose and mouth cover in sand storms. In former times, the *ghutrah/sham'agh* kept a horse or camel rider's long hair from blowing in his face. Most men leave the *ghutrah* or *sham'agh* on at all times except when relaxing at home. It is impolite to ask a Saudi to remove his head covering.

The large square of cotton material is folded diagonally and placed on top of a *taqiyah*, a white skull cap that keeps the hair in place. The *igaal*, a black, braided cord, is doubled over and set on top of the *ghutrah* or *sham'agh*. It is coarse enough to keep a grip on the *ghutrah* or *sham'agh* and prevent slipping. The *igaal* was originally used to hobble camels. King Abdul Aziz and senior tribal and government officials wore a more elaborate *igaal* with three tiers of cord bound together with gold thread and a tassle down the back. King Faisal was the last Saudi monarch to wear this style.

Saudi men traditionally wear a full-length, long-sleeved garment called a *thobe*. Buttons at the neck and the wrist give the *thobe* the appearance of a long shirt. The design of nearly all *thobes* includes deep pockets on the left and right sides. Most also have a breast pocket.

Materials vary from fine cottons to inexpensive polyester. Islam prohibits Muslim men from wearing silk. *Thobes* keep the wearer cool by a chimney effect which draws air in at the bottom and allows it to circulate effectively, unimpeded by tight-waisted apparel. White *thobes* predominate but some men wear heavier materials and darker colours in winter. Lightweight white shorts or long, drawstring pantaloons called *sirwaal* are worn underneath the *thobe*.

For extra warmth during the winter months, some men wear a jacket over their *thobes*; others prefer the elegant, full-length, tailored coat called a *digla*. Throughout the year as a mark of prestige or on occasions demanding dressier attire, the full-length cloak of cream, brown, or black wool or camel hair called a *bisht* or *mishlah* is often worn over the *thobe*. The finely woven fabric and the beautiful edgings of patterned gold braid distinguish the best from the ordinary *bisht*. Because it is so expensive to buy the more elegant *bisht/mishlah*, many men choose to rent them for occasions such as weddings and special ceremonies. Openings in the side seams just below the shoulders allow the wearer's arms to protrude. Usually, however, the cloak rests on the shoulders and the right side is neatly tucked under the left arm. Although the loose, flowing style makes the *bisht* look like a one-size-fits-all garment, each *bisht* is tailored to fit the wearer. Interestingly, they are not shortened at the hemline but at a seam which runs horizontally at approximately knee level.

In particularly cold weather, Saudis wear a *farwa*. The original design of the *farwa* consisted of a single sheepskin. It has evolved into a long, sleeved coat lined with several sheepskins (or synthetic fibres). Like the lighter weight *bisht* or *mishlah*, the *farwa* has no buttons or zippers. A simple geometric pattern often decorates the upper middle back area. The *farwa* is such an effective deterrent against the cold that the bedouin may use it as bedding during the winter.

European-style shoes have crept into Saudi wardrobes, but even the most urbane members of the population keep leather sandals (*na'al*) on hand. The traditional styles usually have plastic threading which joins camel skin soles to colourfully painted goat skin uppers. A layer of camel grease gives them a protective coating. International manufacturers have bowed to market demands and produce chic footwear which is reminiscent of local custom while at the same time is an expression of modern tastes.

In the southwest regions of the Kingdom, many men, particularly the older generation, continue to wear the traditional *djambiya*, a dagger encased in a sharply curved sheath covered with ornately decorated silver or other metal. The dagger is held in place by a leather or colourfully embroidered belt. The *djambiya* is often worn at official or ceremonial functions by men who might not otherwise wear it as a daily addition to their clothing. Carrying custom a step further, some men also wear a bandolier over each shoulder and criss-crossing the chest.

It is against the customs of Islam for Muslim men to wear gold jewellery. Men display their social standing with expensive accessories such as watches, pens, and cufflinks.

Most men also have a string of *sibha* or worry beads. Each bead represents one of the names describing the greatness of Allah. Nowadays they are seldom used as prayer beads. Instead, they keep the right hand occupied and pass the time in a therapeutic manner. In a *majlis* (large gathering), a foreigner without worry beads may sometimes be given a set. Usually this is a temporary loan. The offer to return the beads should be made before the visitor departs. Similarly, someone may suddenly borrow a set of beads, which should be given without comment. Worry beads come in all price ranges and a wide variety of materials, including plastic, wood, metal, and semi-precious stones.

Women

In deference to religious requirement, Muslim women over the age of puberty when appearing in public cover their hair with a black gauze scarf called a *tarha*. From neck to ankle they shroud themselves in a silk or synthetic outer garment called an *abaya*. Islam stipulates that women should dress modestly and hide their shape from anyone who is not a member of the family. In the Gulf region, *abayas* evolved as the response to this religious requirement.

Traditional *abayas* are kept closed by raising each side of the fabric in turn and securing it under the opposite arm. Recently, Westerners have also been obliged to wear the *abaya*. Because they are usually less adept at keeping the front closed while using their arms, the style has evolved to include fastenings which allow more freedom of movement. There is also a trend towards making this otherwise drab covering into a fashion statement incorporating designer diamantés, silver threads, or decorative borders—and even the use of colourful fabric—but the inescapable objective of full concealment remains unaltered.

Underneath the forbidding black, dresses come in as many colours and styles as the mind can imagine. In the main centres of Riyadh, Jeddah, and Dhahran, designer fashions are not uncommon. In smaller cities and rural areas, traditional designs prevail. These full-length, long-sleeved styles may have geometric patterns, colourful appliqué or rich needlework, depending on the region.

In addition, many Saudi women choose to fully veil their faces in public and in private in the presence of non-family males. This is not a result of religious necessity but rather one of personal modesty and local custom. The most common type of facial covering is an unadorned gauze veil. In some areas, leather masks replace the veil. In other areas, women partially veil their faces with a *burqa*. This often heavily decorated mask ties at the back of the head, leaves the forehead bare, and has openings for the eyes. It is worn mostly by women in southwestern tribes.

Saudi women, particularly the bedouin, love to adorn themselves with jewellery. In this society, jewellery is more than mere fashion; it also indicates status and, in times of need, provides a useful source of cash. Traditionally, when a woman dies, her jewellery is melted down. It is considered unsuitable for a new bride to have second-hand jewellery. This explains why relatively few pieces of authentic old jewellery survive.

Within the past 40 years, gold jewellery has become popular but it is still the rustic silver that is so closely associated with bedouin designs. The distinctive, large, heavy pieces are called 'bedouin' jewellery because they were made for the bedouin, not by them. Silversmiths based in communities through which the bedouin passed, usually associated themselves with a particular tribe and designed exclusively for their tastes and needs.

An interesting feature of bedouin jewellery is the fact that the many hanging baubles—coins, balls, beads—serve the purpose of announcing the approach of the wearer with a thythmical jingling sound. This is useful in a society where men and women are segregated. The audible warning allows men time to disappear discreetly.

Foreigners

Any style of clothing is acceptable in the privacy of the home or compound. In public, Western women, even if they are not Muslim, are required to dress conservatively and to refrain from wearing any styles which might cause offence. Modest necklines (to the collar bone), elbow-length sleeves or longer, and mid-calf or full-length hemlines are appropriate. Most women wear an *abaya*. As well as responding to current local custom, it has the advantage of camouflaging otherwise unsuitable clothing such as tight trousers or short skirts. A few women wear shorts or sleeveless tops under their *abayas* but this is not recommended.

It is not a requirement for non-Muslims to cover their hair but many women carry a scarf to minimize the possibility of clashes with *mutawwa* (religious police).

Businessmen generally wear ties and long- or short-sleeved shirts; they often forego the formality of a suit or sports jacket unless they are attending meetings with clients or making courtesy calls. Shirts worn in public should not be open below the collar bone. Shorts should be restricted to homes, compounds, or beaches.

CHAPTER FIVE

SOCIAL CONVENTION

EW FOREIGNERS ARRIVE in Saudi Arabia with more than a smattering of information about the Kingdom's social formalities. In the beginning, the best way to handle most situations is to do whatever is correct in your own society. Saudis show a gracious tolerance towards well-meant *faux pas* but the informed person avoids causing unnecessary, albeit unintentional, offense.

Forms of Address

In Saudi Arabia, a person's name indicates his patrilineal descent. At birth a child is given only one name of his or her own. This precedes the descriptor *ibn* or *bin* (son of) or *bint* (daughter of) followed by the father's name, another *ibn*, *bin* or *bint* and the

grandfather's name, and so on, normally not exceeding four generations. Although confusing to foreigners, the system quickly establishes descent within the large family groupings. Sometimes the *bin/bint* may be dropped but the order of lineage remains constant. This method of classification also proves useful in distinguishing individuals with the same names. For example, in an office there may be several 'Mohammeds' (this is the most common male name on earth). There may even be more than one 'Mohammed' who shares the same family name. It is unlikely, however, that they will share the same second name...and if they do, there is always the third name.

The style of family names indicates tribal origin. People from the south take their family names from villages, such as Zahrani or Gahtani. People from the Hijaz, Saudi Arabia's western province, distinguish themselves with the use of three names only: the person's given name, the father's given name, and the grandfather's given name, as in 'Sarah/Mohammed Yusef Abdullah'. A boy might also be given the additional name of Mohammed or Ahmed before his chosen name. This is believed to bring extra blessings upon the child. In the north of the Kingdom, the tribal name is used without *al* or *bin* preceeding. Because of the history of later settlement and migration, tribes from the Eastern Province have no specific pattern to their names.

Saudis do not normally expect people to stand on ceremony, though respect and care to avoid offense are always in order. A quick departure from introductory titles to first names is typical, not necessarily because of friendship but because this is the given name and the proper name by which a person should be referred.

Mohammed Talal Tamimi is Mr. Mohammed or Mr. Mohammed Talal, not Mr. Talal. This explains why Saudis often preceed the first name with 'Mr.', 'Mrs.', or 'Miss' when addressing foreigners. Foreigners who have reached the informal stage with Saudis might use the term *abu* ('father of') followed by the name of the eldest son, or daughter if there is no son.

The title *Sheikh* (pronounced 'shayk', not 'sheek') is usually given to the leader of a tribe or to a man who has earned stature in the community through age, wealth, or influence. For example, the heads of large trading establishments are usually referred to as *Sheikh* before their first name. Because the title denotes respect, it is sometimes used as a polite form of address or to refer to the revered head of a family. *Tal omrek* is another form of address which shows particular respect. It is the equivalent of 'sir' and is used alone, not before a first name.

Members of the Royal Family normally introduce themselves as (name) bin/bint (name). Unless otherwise instructed, foreigners should address the person as 'Your Royal Highness', 'Your Highness', or 'Prince/Princess (name)'.

Only Saudi princes and princesses who are direct descendants (through the male line) of kings are referred to as 'Royal Highness' (HRH); other members of the Al-Saud family are referred to as 'Highness' (HH). Official correspondence should bear the correct title and full name. The letter's salutation can read 'Dear Prince (first name)' or 'Your [Royal] Highness'.

Government ministers are referred to as 'Excellency', although this title may be dropped quite quickly once a relationship develops. It is also a useful salutation in formal situations where there has been no opportunity to establish the correct titles of senior Saudis.

Because names reflect geneology, women always retain their own family names (given name, *bint* father's name, *bin* grandfather's name, etc.), even after marriage. To facilitate introductions in Western society, a wife is often referred to as Mrs. (husband's last name). It is correct, however, to introduce her simply by her first name, without 'Mrs.' "This is Sarah, the wife of Mohammed (last name)" or "This is Ibrahim and his wife Sarah."

Friendship

Friendship with a Saudi brings with it the responsibilities of unwavering loyalty and an unfaltering willingness to be of assistance. These duties are both expected from and given to friends. Saudis are usually willing to inconvenience themselves in order to assist a friend. At the very least, it is necessary to give a convincing appearance that an attempt will be made. Giving and receiving favours is part of the equation of friendship but close relationships are seldom formed on this basis alone.

Saudis tend not to make a distinction between 'business associates' and 'friends'. Good personal relationships, therefore, contribute significantly to good business relationships.

Westerners, who often tend to be more aloof by nature, sometimes find the frequent contact of Arab associates overwhelming. Good friends visit each other regularly and talk on the phone at least every few days. Privacy in the Western sense is alien to the Saudi, although Westernized

Saudis normally call before dropping in on Western friends. Saudis are most appreciative of a foreign friend's attentiveness.

Men openly hold hands in Saudi Arabia. It is usually a sign of amity, seldom a sexual overture. Foreign men may feel uncomfortable with such a display but it would be insensitive to prematurely withdraw from the contact.

Male-Female Saudi-Expat Relationships

There exists a mutual misunderstanding between Saudi men and expat women. Some men think that Western women possess a moral laxity which at best equals that of floozy film stars. Many expat women, on the other hand, suspect that, given half a chance, Saudi men will make unwanted sexual advances. While these stereotypes do exist, most would agree that they are the exception rather than the rule. Yet these two incorrect extremes of opinion persist and, in many circles, prevail. Consequently, unless he has been introduced, the normally respectful Saudi man is reluctant to speak with or look at Western women who all too often have been misadvised not to make eye contact with Saudi men. Neither of these extremes is necessary if discreet and courteous behaviour is displayed.

The moral reputation of women is not more important in the Saudi culture than in other cultures, it is simply perceived differently. Foreign men should never approach Saudi women unless they already know each other. Even then, discretion is advised in case the action is misinterpreted by observers.

Foreigners should also be circumspect in their behaviour towards each other. Public displays of affection are offensive to Saudis. Couples should refrain from holding hands and prolonged touching. Under no circumstances should they exchange romantic kisses in public. Even the innocent and generally accepted greeting kiss can result in arrest if witnessed by the wrong individual.

Saving Face

Saudis often go to extreme lengths to resolve problems without conflict or embarrassment. 'Saving face' is an important feature of the culture; honour, reputation, and dignity are vitally important and nothing must be allowed to threaten them. Reality, therefore, may be reconstructed in order to save face. Westerners who fail to understand this aspect of the Arab personality will face constant frustration in inter-cultural relationships and will probably suffer subtle obstructions in their business dealings.

Saudis will be impressively creative in their methods to allow a person to tactfully extricate himself from an awkward situation. Nor will a Saudi admit to wrongdoing if in doing so it compromises his dignity. In interactions with Saudis, foreigners should be aware of this cultural imperative and behave with consideration. If a confrontation is unavoidable, this is best done in private with only the person concerned.

Another facet of saving face is the reluctance to say 'no'. This desire to co-operate can be seen as an offshoot of hospitality and friendship: it is rude to refuse anything to a guest or a friend. Inevitably, verbal commitments may exceed capabilities. It it impolite to refuse a request outright. Be aware that a positive response is not necessarily the same as a positive result. It is better not to expect or insist on things which could prove to be unreasonable. If words have not been translated into action within a reasonable period of time, it is safe to assume that a positive conclusion is unlikely. Don't risk the relationship by pushing too much.

Gift Giving

An Arab considers stinginess to be one of the most distasteful of reputations. Generosity, on the other hand, is a virtue accorded great esteem. Saudi generosity can go to seemingly inexhaustible lengths. When and how should a foreigner reciprocate?

The primary occasions for gifts are the *'eid* holidays at the end of Ramadan and *hajj* (when only children receive presents), weddings, and births. At these times foreigners do not usually offer gifts unless they have developed a close friendship with a Saudi family.

Expatriates are frequently invited to share the happiness of a wedding celebration despite the fact that they might not know the bride or groom. In such circumstances, gifts are not usually expected. Close friends and family offer gifts a few days after the night of the wedding party.

Traditionally, Saudis simply 'remember' birthdays. Nowadays, however, there is a growing trend to celebrate children's birthdays with Western-style parties. If invited to such an event, bring a present.

Businessmen should refrain from offering gifts at a first meeting or when alone with the intended recipient. These gestures could be interpreted as bribery and as such are offensive—and illegal. Although there is a risk of indebtedness in accepting gifts, there is a greater likelihood of causing offense—and perhaps damaging a fledgling business relationship—in refusing gifts. If refusal is necessary it should be handled graciously and diplomatically, allowing the Saudi to save face.

Gifts for children are always enthusiastically received. Except between close friends, it is unacceptable for a man to give a gift to a Saudi gentleman for his wife, no matter how innocent the intention.

When visiting a Saudi family, it is courteous (but not necessary) to bring a small gift.

It is generally advisable to refrain from offering presents which depict human or animal forms as these are perceived by many Saudis as un-Islamic.

Saudis accept gifts gratefully but it is not customary for them to overtly display their appreciation, nor will they usually open the gift until after the guest has left.

More perplexing than when and if to give gifts is when and how to accept them. Gift-giving is an important attribute in the Saudi culture but their munificence often overwhelms foreigners who are uncomfortable recipients of 'windfall' largesse. To avoid embarrassment, foreigners should not show too much admiration for a Saudi's possessions. An enthusiastic compliment is welcome but prolonged praise might make the Saudi feel compelled to offer the item under discussion. Sometimes Saudis make such an offer regardless of the degree of comment simply because they inherently enjoy the pleasure of giving. A potential recipient who truly feels uncomfortable about accepting an item should employ a clever combination of tact and charm in refusing. This will hopefully allow the benevolent Saudi to keep his possession without losing face. If the Saudi remains insistent, then accept graciously and at some point in the future present him/her with something special, although this is by no means necessary or expected. The important thing to remember is never to become rude or impatient. Kindness and sincerity inspire the offer; try to respond accordingly.

Gestures

Saudis find it offensive to sit across from someone who overtly exposes the soles of his shoes. Businessmen who are in the habit of putting their feet on their desks should never do so in front of a Saudi visitor. It is equally unacceptable to use some idiomatic references to shoes, such as 'Put yourself in my shoes'.

In the presence of royalty or senior officials, it is a mark of respect to sit with the legs uncrossed.

The use of the raised forefinger to beckon someone can be misinterpreted. Instead, turn the hand palm downward and move all the fingers at once.

Pursing all the fingers together, palm upward, and making a small movement with the wrist is used to convey a command of patience. The words *shway, shway* (slowly, slowly) often accompany the gesture.

Language

The true heritage of Arabia can be found in its language. In the nomadic culture, words could be carried without burden. In the harsh desert environment which was not conducive to the development of fine arts, the cultivation of language became an art form in itself. The immense power, beauty, and range of Arabic makes it one of history's greatest literary languages. Even today, poetry and eloquence hold a revered place in Saudi culture.

Spoken Arabic is not merely a tool for conceptualization, it is a vehicle to convey atmosphere and emotion. Add to this the rich vocabulary and the often ritual patterns of address and it is not hard to understand why it may take longer to express an idea in Arabic than in most other languages. Conversely, a single Arabic word can encompass complex philosophical, even military, concepts.

Spoken Arabic brings with it an elaborate set of mannerisms which may be confusing to a foreigner. Hands wave, voices rise, phrases are repeated—repeatedly—and oaths and blessings (but not curses and obscenities) are liberally sprinkled throughout the conversation. All this usually just indicates a cultural quirk, not negative aggression. In fact, foreigners who make their point only once, and who do so in a calm, controlled manner, may have their sincerity questioned!

In order not to encourage any form of bad luck, superstitious Arabs tend to speak in euphemisms, substituting vague words and phrases for more explicit descriptions. For example, a person with a serious illness might be referred to as being 'tired'.

Next to cultural awareness and respect, nothing makes a foreigner more welcome than an attempt to learn Arabic. It is not an easy language. The grammar is complex, the vocabulary is extensive, and even the alphabet is not entirely straightforward. Some of the 28 characters represent different pronunciations of the same letter. A few of the sounds are strongly guttural and must be formed at the back of the throat, a considerable challenge for most students of the language.

In addition to the numerous dialects and copious vocabulary, there are three families of Arabic: Classical, the seventh century language of the *Quran*, and the format for written Arabic and such formalities as speeches; Standard Literary, used in the media and as a common communication between different dialects; and Spoken, the colloquial form distinct to each region. While geographic regions have their own dialects, such as Gulf or Egyptian, within these areas vocabulary and pronunciation can differ considerably. An Arab from one country cannot necessarily understand or be understood by someone from another country where Arabic is the main language, although they would both normally have recourse to the classical language if necessary.

Taking all these difficulties into consideration, the novice will find his most hesitant and clumsy efforts warmly appreciated. Increased grammatical capabilities provide valuable insights into local perspectives. This inevitably enriches a stay in the Kingdom and often opens doors to the culture which might otherwise remain closed.

Written Arabic, with its many graceful curves and swirls, lends itself to the art of calligraphy. The elegance of the script can be appreciated even by those who do not understand the meaning of the words. The script is written from right to left.

All official correspondence with government bodies in Saudi Arabia must be in Arabic.

Numbers

Although Arabic script is read from right to left, numbers are read from left to right. The pattern is slightly complicated when there are hyphenated numbers. For example the Arabic numerals 123-456 would actually be read as 456-123. Each block of numbers before or after the hyphen is read as a total unit using a left to right sequence. "456" is read before "123" because it falls under the right to left rule used for script. A frequent confusion over telephone numbers illustrates this problem!

Non-Arabs tend to refer to numbers written in Arabic script as 'Arabic numbers'. In fact, the Arabs had no number system of their own; they first adopted and then, through the spread of Islam, disseminated the Hindu pure place value system. The use of decimals and zeros made it faster and easier to solve complex mathematical problems. Originally written in Sanskrit, the Hindi numbers were gradually modified to suit the Arabic script. Western numerals are adapted from the Arabic style.

1 2 3 4 5 6 7 8 9 0

١ ٢ ٣ ٤ ٥ ٦ ٧ ٨ ٩ .

Photography

Photography remains a sensitive subject in Saudi Arabia. Discretion and approval are advised at all times. Do not photograph local people, particularly women, without first asking permission. Photographers who ignore such courtesies risk an encounter with local authorities who may confiscate their film. Professional photographers should obtain official permission from local government offices before beginning a shoot. This permission comes in the form of a letter placed in a sealed enveloped with an official government stamp. The envelope is seldom if ever opened because the stamp provides the necessary assurance to the general public that the exercise has been sanctioned by those in charge.

Once agreement has been given, photographers will usually find that Saudis are enthusiastic subjects. Children, especially, love to have their pictures taken. A Polaroid camera can be a useful accessory. The thrill of an 'instant' picture serves as a special thank you.

Military installations, airports, and government structures (including palace gates), are strictly off limits to photographers without prior approval.

CHAPTER SIX

BARGAINING

THE ENVIABLE SKILL of bargaining seems inherent to the Arab personality. This instinct to negotiate surfaces at every opportunity and is a stimulating feature of day-to-day life in Saudi Arabia.

Whether making a high-powered deal in the boardroom or bartering at the *suq*, the fundamental techniques are similar. Both circumstances require tenacity, finesse, and, most importantly, the right attitude.

Saudis greet the prospect of bargaining with enthusiasm and as a chance to match wits. Reaching an agreement is a game they play to win, but with as much proficiency and good grace as possible.

During the opening gestures of exchanging greetings, a good negotiator establishes eye contact in an effort to appraise the 'opponent'—who of course uses the same techniques to try to gain advantage. Each looks into the other's eyes, searching for hints of strength and weakness.

Because clever negotiating is such an agreeable pastime, Saudis often prolong the occasion. It is discourteous to begin any bargaining or business discussions without first completing the ritual greetings and social dialogue. Depending on the circumstances, the period may extend to coffee or even sharing a meal. Business negotiations, particularly, can take days or weeks...or sometimes years. Foreigners unfamiliar with such lengthy procedures feel frustrated until they learn to adapt. Closing a deal in an allotted time frame is less effective in the long run than succeeding with a tolerant attitude and appreciation for the time-honoured tradition of protracted negotiations.

Retail Bargaining

The local *suqs* provide the most basic school for bargaining. Here, skills are sharpened by haggling over a kilo of tomatoes or a few grams of gold. Novices who overcome their initial inhibitions quickly learn to enjoy Saudi-style shopping—after they master some fundamental points.

First and foremost, it is essential to know the value of the item being negotiated. Only then can you bargain from a position of strength. Sometimes, however, this is not possible, so a good rule of thumb is that whether or not a quote sounds outrageous, the initial figure usually exceeds the accepted market value of the item, except in 'fixed price' establishments.

How do you arrive at the 'right' price? Some people assume that the first quote represents an inflation of about 20% over what they eventually will pay. Not wishing to prolong the banter, they immediately make an offer in the region of the anticipated final price.

Other people prefer to start at the bottom end of the scale. They volunteer to pay only about 20% of the initial asking price. After mock rejections, the vendor grudgingly lowers the price and the purchaser sympathetically increases his offer until finally they arrive at a mutually agreeable amount somewhere in between. Traders normally try to get more from an expat because not only do Westerners have higher incomes, they probably would pay more for the item in their own countries.

Some foreigners feel embarrassed about bargaining but in this culture it is standard practice, particularly when buying more than one item. Often, if a potential buyer does not bargain, the vendor will assume he's not serious and will move on to another customer. The reverse is also true: Saudis often think that a vendor who is not interested in bargaining actually has no intention of selling or else that he wants to overcharge his customers.

Try not to express enthusiasm or admiration for a desired item as this gives the vendor an advantage and will inevitably make the opening price higher. With a detached

manner, study several items in the same vicinity. The vendor's uncertainty works in the customer's favour.

One tactic used by foreigners to lower the price is to point out a flaw (real or imagined). Saudis, on the other hand, tell the merchant that his item is too good for them and that they can't possibly afford to buy it.

Despite the shopkeeper's argument that the goods cost him more than you are offering, don't be fooled—or shamed—into untimely concessions. Remember, however, that the merchant has a right to earn a decent living.

Of course, there is more to good bargaining than mere haggling. The best bargainers instinctively employ tact, courtesy, subtlety, and infinite patience. In sophisticated negotiations, price may not even be discussed on the first visit.

Good bargainers know when to smile at a preposterous bid, when to put on expressions of shock or dismay, when to pretend to walk away, and when to really walk away. Most importantly, they know not to take themselves or the negotiations so seriously that they forget to enjoy the experience. Remember that bargaining is most successful when both parties feel satisfied with the deal. The encounter should never be spoiled by becoming a contest of wills.

After the price has been agreed, the effort is often rewarded with a complimentary gift. (Foreigners usually refer to this as *baksheesh* but this choice of wording actually has negative connotations of bribery.) The gift symbolizes a confirmation of friendship. Whether offered by the vendor or asked for by the purchaser, it makes the deal a little sweeter. Saudis are not just good at negotiating, they are also adept at commercial psychology!

Business Negotiations

Saudis are tough negotiators; this trait becomes magnified when a relatively inexperienced expat is involved. Reminiscent of the old Arab trading mentality, paragraphs in Saudi-originated contracts may be heavily weighted in the Saudi's favour—and will remain so unless negotiations achieve otherwise. Experience has taught Saudis to be suspicious.

Foreigners who enter into business negotiations in Saudi Arabia usually need to prove the quality of their products or services in order to justify prices which may seem excessive. Bringing a deal to a successful conclusion is usually considerably more challenging and time consuming than an excursion to the *suqs*!

Inevitably, concessions must be granted. Pricing is an obvious starting point. Allow some 'wiggle' room but be careful not to inflate the initial price to such an extent that the potential customer/client questions the true value of the item on offer. If pricing can no longer be restructured, try reducing the size of the package. This lowers cost without compromising integrity.

Although courtesy is always an important ingredient in dealings, be prepared for a show of exaggerated emotion. This is part of the theatre of bargaining. If your offer is fair, don't be intimidated into conceding your position.

Be alert to recognizing when negotiations are going nowhere. Arabs consider an outright rejection inhospitable and so may endure several meetings, each time offering polite delays on decisions. Eventually, the salesman/businessman will realize his endeavours are wasting everyone's time and give up—without the Saudi having had to say 'no'.

CHAPTER SEVEN

DOING BUSINESS

T IS 10:15 A.M. You have had three cups of cardamom coffee, countless cups of sweet Arabic tea, five cigarettes, and read the morning paper twice from cover to cover. You have also travelled 5,000 miles and had less than five hours of sleep in the past 28 hours. All this so you would be on time for your 9:00 a.m. appointment. The Saudi businessman with whom you have your meeting only has to come across town. The office secretary keeps saying he should arrive any minute; the tea boy winks and says the boss never appears before 11:00 a.m. Frustration overpowers you.

Nowadays the above scenario is the exception rather than the rule but it remains a possibility. Most Saudi businessmen are involved in several often diverse business activities and may work out of more than one office. Delays, although unintended, are sometimes unavoidable...and they often occur without benefit of forewarning. Extra time allotments in business agendas allow for unexpected or rescheduled meetings.

Saudis, moreover, are generally less hampered by the finite approach to time which most Westerners have. Individuals on tight schedules can find an encounter with this attitude annoying and unproductive but a loss of temper will do little to change inherent habits. On the contrary, it could damage a fledgling relationship.

It is wise to remember the Saudi tendency towards 'no confrontation' (see Chapter 5). A Saudi businessman might agree to an appointment with a persistent individual simply because he does not want to offend him by saying 'no'; however, it is unlikely that he will cancel other commitments despite his apparent acquiescence.

The regularly repeated expression *Insha'allah* (if it is God's will) has come to have negative, or at best non-urgent, connotations for most foreigners, especially businessmen who interpret the phrase as "Don't hold your breath waiting". In fact, there is nothing negative—or positive—about the word. It quite simpy means that the speaker puts his full faith in God and that he is an obedient instrument of His will. To jest about something which Muslims consider to be an unassailable truth is both insensitive and offensive.

Even business appointments which are on time can be disconcerting for foreign businessmen. They may find that they have to share the meeting with telephone calls on several lines and with a constant stream of people wandering in and out of the office. This is the *majlis* syndrome. Among the bedouin, anyone can come to the leader's tent to exchange news, recite poetry, discuss problems, settle disputes, or present petitions. The same procedure prevails in the homes of urban dignitaries. Today this custom of easy accessibility still survives, whether it be with tribal leaders, corporate executives, or members of the Royal Family. It takes experience to become adept at conducting preliminary business meetings in these circumstances. Business deals are not concluded in this environment. The serious stages of negotiations are discussed in private.

Onc consolation is that thc systcm can work *for* businessmen, not just against them. This is particularly so when it suddenly becomes necessary to see an official and there is no time to make a proper appointment. Normally, foreigners should not appear unannounced at a Saudi's office, particularly at the offices of senior executives, but the *majlis* makes exceptions acceptable.

Introductions

Trust is a vital feature of successful business ventures in Saudi Arabia. This is particularly true in dealings with foreigners. The boom years of the 1970s saw too many fly-by-night profiteers who absconded with large sums of money or conveniently disappeared when things went wrong. Caution now prevails and confidence must be earned.

Because trust usually takes time to establish, contacts and introductions are invaluable, especially to a businessman who makes only sporadic visits to the Kingdom. With the right recommendation, a foreigner has the advantage of being welcomed with an openness that otherwise might not become apparent for several meetings, if ever. Since introductions reflect relationships, a Saudi businessman is likely to be cautious about whom he introduces to possible competitors.

In order to make full use of valuable introductions, the foreign businessman must be prepared to devote time and energy towards building and sustaining the new relationship. 'Being there' is an important aspect in the development of trust. Businessmen who come to Saudi Arabia for short periods every few months cannot hope to have the ongoing success which is more likely as a result of regular, prolonged visits—or residency.

Business Attitudes

Discretion: The Saudi's strong inclination towards privacy is evident in his approach to business. Knowledge is guarded jealously and confidentiality is expected. Saudis will not discuss important business in front of or with people whom it does not concern. Foreigners are advised to be discerning in the disclosure of information about themselves and their business partners. Saudis shy away from people who lack discretion.

Occupations: When asked what he does, a Saudi may not divulge a specific job title or profession. Vague descriptions such as 'in business' or 'in government' are common. This is not a smoke screen. Many Saudis are involved, actively and/or silently, in a number of diverse businesses. To list a full range of activities would possibly be time consuming and probably sound boastful. It is easier to generalize. Modesty and discretion also influence the giving of information. Someone 'in government' might be a minister or he could be a minor technician. Those who need to know, know; others can judge at face value. Do not cross the fine line into prying. A business card may give more details. Discreet enquiries through contacts usually provide adequate background.

Relationships: Most Saudis align themselves to an individual of 'superior' importance and influence. A superior's followers will include a wider cross-section of the social strata than would normally be seen in Western societies. In exchange for safeguarding the welfare of his supporters, a superior figure expects loyalty, honour, and obedience. In business, a superior is expected to be authoritative. A direct request for a subordinate's opinion would be interpreted as a display of weakness. Nevertheless, a good superior will respect the uniqueness of each individual. Ideally, treatment is equal but different.

Because of the tribal nature of Saudi society, the concept of 'conflict of interest' has little relevance in this part of the world. It is expected that those in a position to do so will look after those in need.

Praise/Criticism: Saudis go to great length to avoid being strongly critical. Similarly, they take it as an affront to their dignity and self-esteem if someone criticizes them directly, particularly if this is done in front of others. Criticisms should be couched in indirect phrases and should not come until the person has first had positive points highlighted. Praise is always appreciated but in the Arab relationship it is a necessity.

Emotion/Logic: The Arab race bubbles over with a wide range of emotions which are enthusiastically aired at every opportunity. Logic-oriented foreigners are bewildered when the introduction of reason fails to achieve the anticipated result. It is always useful in negotiations to introduce personal elements of persuasion, for example, calling on friendships and abilities, demonstrating charm and, if possible, eloquence. A lack of emotion and unwavering logic seldom appeal to the more colourful psyche of the Saudi.

Advertising: The traditional Saudi distrusts advertising. He feels that if a company has to advertise then it probaby isn't doing well. Despite the emergence of sophisticated public relations, marketing, and advertising firms which reflect the Kingdom's growing awareness of the commercial viability of positive public perception, word of mouth remains the most effective marketing strategy.

Basic Courtesies

Foreigners tend to separate business from pleasure. Saudis never like to dispense with the exchange of courtesies. Sometimes the period of 'small talk' can seem protracted according to Western custom but to rush the ritual is insensitive and possibly detrimental. Foreigners should be aware that this social interaction also serves an 'investigative' purpose. The answers to seemingly innocuous questions can provide potentially useful business data.

Just as Saudis don't like to rush introductory conversation, they don't like to be pressured into arriving at business decisions. Backing them into a corner or introducing time constraints seldom works to the foreigner's advantage. There are a variety of reasons why responses can be slow in coming: superiors may have to be consulted, facts may have to be verified, relationships may have to be strengthened, or the Saudi may simply not want to refuse outright and thereby cause offense. Business deals here take time and repeated visits. Even with such an investment of patience, the conclusion may not be satisfactory to the foreigner.

Saudis understandably find it offensive to sit opposite a foreign businessman who has a superior attitude and is inflexible. Expatriates who take the time to listen and to accommodate and compromise where necessary not only win respect but also often have the greatest business successes.

Business cards should be printed in English on one side and Arabic on the other. It's a good idea to have an Arab colleague check the Arabic for misspellings and misinterpretations of the pronunciation of names.

Although most presentations by foreign companies are in English, it is a courtesy to provide presentation documents in both English and Arabic. Have a trusted person carefully check the translation for inaccuracies.

At the end of a meeting, visitors are shown special honour if the Saudi host walks them to the door. Saudis appreciate it when foreigners accord them similar attention.

Business Hours

Offices generally start work around 0800h. Foreign companies often work straight through the day and finish at 1700h. Most Arab companies work a split shift, taking a break of several hours in the afternoon and returning in the late afternoon or early evening for a couple of hours. In the Eastern Province, many businesses begin around 0700h, work straight through, and finish around 1600h.

Except for the large supermarkets which are open 24 hours, most stores are open by 0930h. They close for the midday prayer and then open again at 1600h. Most remain open (except during prayer) until 2200h. The shops that elect to open on Fridays do so from 1600h.

Ramadan ushers in total confusion in business hours. In the absence of a government directive to bring conformity to the situation, each company and shop decides its own hours. The only consistency is that all shops are open from 2030h to at least midnight. Some stay open until 0200h. Offices are generally open from at least 1000h-1400h and sometimes in the evenings as well. It's necessary to check ahead of Ramadan to find out the hours of each company/store where you're likely to do business.

The business week in Saudi Arabia is from Saturday to Wednesday, although a number of private companies work at least half a day on Thursday and a few even work the full day. Unless it's a matter of urgency, neither Saudis nor expatriate workers appreciate being disturbed with business matters on Friday, the Saudi equivalent of Sunday. This effectively limits the productive work week to only four days but head offices in other parts of the world should respect the need for Saudi-based employees to have a day off!

When to Visit

October to June is the most popular period for business trips. The temperatures usually do not reach unbearable levels and it is safely before or after the summer exodus.

Businessmen try to avoid visiting the Kingdom during

Ramadan, a holy month (*see* Chapters 12 and 15) in which Muslims fast during daylight hours. Office hours are abbreviated during the day and are often extended to evening hours—sometimes well into the evening. Foreign businessmen who maintain their regular office hours can find Ramadan rigorous if they also attend late-night meetings. Saudis themselves show signs of strain or lethargy in the latter part of Ramadan. Because of the demands of fasting, important decisions are often delayed until after *'eid*.

During the *'eid* holidays at the end of Ramadan and *hajj*, offices remain closed for at least four days and as long as two weeks in government or government-related concerns and some other Saudi companies. These celebrations follow the lunar calendar, so they occur 11 days earlier each year.

CHAPTER EIGHT

FAMILY

HE SAUDI CONSIDERS his family deserving of the greatest loyalty. This exceeds obligations to tribes, rulers, friends, and employers, a fact which is understandable and acceptable to Saudis but often causes difficulties in foreign-run businesses.

'Family' in the Arab sense extends beyond the immediate relatives to include even the most remote members of a common tribe. A Saudi does not see himself as an individual as much as part of a whole: the family and, to a lesser extent, the tribe. His responsibilities are to the group rather than to himself. Family pressure to avoid bringing dishonour onto the family is ever present. Shame (disappointing the group) is a more likely emotion than guilt (self-recrimination).

The entire culture is based on kinship, so roots are all-important. Saudis are ultimately judged by their backgrounds and not by financial status. A family's history of such intangibles as generosity, courage, and honour are far more meaningful than the current success or failure of individual members, although this, too, will be woven into the tribe's reputation. Family ties are ingrained from an early age and take precedence over any other obligations or relationships. Although there may be disagreements or even animosities within a family grouping, these are overlooked when it becomes necessary to band together to defend the family honour. An Arab proverb proclaims, *My brothers and I against our cousin; my cousin and I against the stranger.*

Many Saudis, particularly in rural areas, continue the tradition of the extended family, where it is not uncommon for three generations to live together under the same roof. Depending on the size of the house, unmarried children and married sons with their wives and children may live with the parents, at least until the sons become established and start their own homes. In cities, where greater employment opportunities offer increased possibilities of financial independence, there is a growing trend towards smaller, nuclear families.

The eldest male is the head of the family or tribal unit but a father of a sub-family heads his own household. He is responsible for its economic and social well-being, although he relies on support and advice from family members beyond his jurisdiction. The eldest son is the second most important person in a family. He is entrusted with everything, usually to the exclusion of his siblings.

In domestic matters women rule, with the eldest female having the greatest influence. Mothers are accorded special respect, as reflected in the Arabic saying, *The way to paradise is through obedience to mothers.*

Saudi families tend to be large. In conversation, Saudis frequently refer to 'cousins'. There can be so many 'cousins' that foreigners sometimes assume it is a catch-all word used as a substitute for 'brother', 'uncle', or 'friend'. Usually, however, the terminology is perfectly apt. Large families produce numerous cousins!

It is inevitable that foreigners who interact with Saudis will discuss their families. Foreigners who have negative things to say about their background or about any family members should refrain from saying anything at all. This smacks of a certain disloyalty and is incomprehensible to the Saudi.

Children

Saudis have great love for children. It is not unusual for them to approach children they don't know and give them a kiss or a fond pat on the head. They greet childbirth with immense joy, considering it a special gift from God. *May you have many children* is a common blessing.

The birth of the first child often comes within a year of marriage. Some newlyweds wait a bit longer to start their family but they are still in the minority.

The festive occasion of childbirth is marked by the slaughter of a sheep in thanksgiving. Family and friends congratulate the new mother in the hospital and present her with gifts.

One week after a child's birth, the infant is given a name and, if a boy, is circumcised. The parents receive special recognition with the new term of address, *om* (mother) or *abu* (father), preceding the first-born son's name.

Occasionally this applies instead to the birth of a first daughter (until the birth of the first son).

Islam takes the legitimacy of children very seriously. A child born after only six months of marriage is still considered legitimate. Abortion is infrequent and not unanimously accepted. The more liberal school of thought permits it up to the fourth month. After this 'quickening of the embryo', abortion is legal only if the mother's life is in danger.

Adoption as it is known in Western countries is unrecognized in Saudi Arabia. If, for whatever reason, it becomes necessary to place a child with others, they must be as closely related to the child as possible. In the case of foundlings, the child is cared for 'in trust'. He/she becomes a 'client' of the new parents, a 'brother in faith'.

Saudi children mature early. Two-year-olds already have minor social responsibilities and participate in most family activities. By the age of five they can perform a number of useful tasks, and at eight have become junior adults, often entrusted with looking after younger siblings. At this stage the boys begin to spend more time with their fathers.

From the earliest age, children are taught to show respect for adults. They greet their elders with a handshake and a kiss, engage in conversation, and do not interrupt or contradict.

The constant interaction between children and large numbers of appropriate adult role models ensures that traditions are passed down and obligations are clearly defined. Adolescents in rural areas seem to have little difficulty adjusting to the transition into adulthood. Increasingly, the youth in cities face the pull of the Western freedoms. This often puts them in conflict with traditional family members.

Women

In Islamic law, two women equal one man when acting as witnesses or in certain proceedings concerning inheritance. This system allows women corroboration in matters in which they have no experience.

Saudi women enjoy independent powers over their personal possessions. Legally they control their inheritance, private property, and marriage dowry.

It is the responsibility of male family members to support the women and attend to their well-being. This justifies the law of inheritance that a man inherits twice as much as a woman.

The tendency of Saudi women to restrict themselves to the home is slowly changing. Improved educational opportunities and increasing social awareness see growing numbers of women working. Because of the custom of segregation of the sexes, many women prefer to work in female-only environments such as education, social services, and women's banks. Others run their own successful businesses or have made a name for themselves in artistic pursuits. As Saudi women continue to prove their capabilities, their enormous potential will become more widely recognized and accepted.

The recently won 'liberation' of Western women commonly inspires the assumption that Saudi women suffer the same injustice as they once suffered. Foreigners should take into consideration the fact that they view the situation from a different perspective than Saudi women. The Saudi woman's life is markedly different from that of a Western woman. Western women should not equate 'different' with oppressive and unacceptable. Expatriates who take the time to explore the question with Saudi women might be surprised to find how distasteful many of them find Western 'liberation'.

CHAPTER NINE

COURTSHIP AND MARRIAGE

ARRIAGE BRINGS MUCH honour and joy to the Saudi family. When they marry, 'children' become adults. Courtship as it is known in the West does not exist in Saudi society. Here, with few exceptions, marriages are arranged by female family members. Traditional Arabs believe that marriage should foster love rather than be a result of love. Primary considerations in the negotiations are financial security and status within the community.

Minors may marry but the union cannot be consummated until the partners reach majority. For girls this is puberty; boys must be 14 years of age. Such marriages require the permission of the court and the consent of the girl's lawful guardian. This custom was historically a rare occurrence and is even more uncommon today.

In former times it was important to maintain the strength of the family and prevent dilution of both blood and assets. The ideal marriage was considered to be between first cousins. An old Arab expression says, *Marrying a strange woman is like drinking water from an earthenware bottle; marriage with a cousin is like a drink from a dish—you are aware of what you drink.* The offspring of close friends provide an alternate choice. Recent studies indicate a growing trend for young men and women to marry outside their circle of relatives.

The closest adult male relative (as long as he is Muslim) or a reliable member of the community ensures that the proposed union will not bring dishonour to the families. After the prospective partners have passed scrutiny by both families, the man's relatives make a proposal. Islam does not allow forced marriages. The silence of a virgin indicates both modesty and consent. Widows and divorcées must agree to the marriage verbally.

The Marriage Contract and Dowry

When the woman accepts, a premarital contract *(milkah)* is drawn up and witnessed by two competent adults. It stipulates the amount of the dowry *(mahr)* and, occasionally, other conditions, all of which must be adhered to. The terms must be recorded with a judge (*qadhi*) in order for them to be binding in the event of divorce.

The dowry is intended to provide for the bride's financial security. On a more symbolic level, *mahr* serves to compensate the girl and her family for their mutual 'loss'. The social standing of the bride and the relationship between her family and that of the groom determines the size of the *mahr*. Closely related families request only modest payments, while distant relations or unrelated families often demand considerably higher payments. Because the *mahr* can create an excessive burden on the groom and his family, the government encourages the adoption of a standard fee.

Before Islam, dowries were paid to the bride's relatives or guardians. The *Quran*, however, decrees that the groom must pay the dowry in a lump sum directly to the bride before the marriage. If the groom should die, his executors must discharge this duty before all others from his estate.

Islamic law has no community of property, so the dowry and any post-marital acquisitions belong solely to the wife. She can use them in any way she sees fit, although she may voluntarily return all or part to her husband.

The Marriage

Signature or oral ratification of the marriage contract legally sanctions the union. A *qadhi* conducts the ceremony. This official marriage normally takes place in the bride's home with the relatives of the bride and groom in attendance, although the men remain segregated from the women. Even the bride and groom are in separate rooms and the *qadhi* goes from one to the other asking the groom and a representative of the bride if they accept each other. Once it has been established that there is no objection to the marriage, the paperwork is attended to.

Matrimony does not diminish the importance of family ties and lineage. A woman does not take her husband's name when she marries, but keeps her own identity.

Consummation might take place on the day of the wedding or be delayed for days, weeks, or months. Nevertheless, the marriage is considered binding as soon as the contract has been signed. Even if the couple decides to dissolve the marriage before consummation, they must officially divorce.

Men and women celebrate the marriage separately and in different ways. The men gather for a large dinner after *isha* prayer and leave early. The women's wedding party is a festive occasion with music, dancing, singing, food, beverages, and incense which continues into the small hours of the morning. The bride and groom arrive at the women's party around midnight. Their arrival is signalled by the shrill sounds of *zaghareet*, the rapid vibration of the tongue against the back of the upper teeth while holding a high-pitched note. To increase the ululation, the woman might tap four fingers of the right hand on the mouth. Seated on elevated chairs, the bride and groom accept the congratulations and good wishes of the guests.

Some wedding parties continue for four days but the groom appears with the bride only on the first night. Until recently, families held the parties at home. Now the functions more commonly occur in hotels or purpose-built wedding halls.

After the celebration, the couple is escorted to their new home. The groom throws coins to the accompanying children and presents the adults with gifts. His mother-in-law is given jewellery or cash in return for unveiling her face to him.

In the most traditional families, the wedding night is the first time that the newlyweds are alone together. The bride often wears green as a sign of fertility. The following morning, the groom offers his wife a special gift *(subhah)* of gold or jewellery to commemorate the occasion.

Because of their penchant for privacy, Saudis never publicize betrothals and marriages, even when the bride or groom is a prominent citizen.

Who May Marry Whom

Saudis consider it a duty to marry but there are certain restrictions on the choice of partner. If possible, the social and economic status of the couple should be equal or within a prescribed range. In some families, to marry outside the accepted limits is cause for ostracism. In any match, the husband must keep his wife in the style to which she was accustomed—or better.

As desirable as social equality may be, religious equality in marriage is even more important, especially among the *Shiite* sect. Muslims may marry only other Muslims or 'believers in the book,' i.e. Christians or Jews. Inter-faith marriage is not encouraged. In the event that it does occur, the non-Muslim spouse may not inherit from the Muslim spouse. In such cases, conversion to Islam is common. Under no circumstances may a Muslim woman marry a non-Muslim man, although a Muslim man may marry a non-Muslim woman. In this case, the non-Muslim woman can retain her own religion but their children must be brought up as Muslims.

Muslim men are permitted to have four wives at any one time but the women cannot be related to each other. Islam obliges the man to treat each wife equally in every way.

For many reasons, not least of which are financial, polygamy is becoming less prevalent in Saudi society.

Adult widows or divorced women have slightly more freedom than first-time brides. They may choose their own husbands and negotiate the marriage contract. However, if they are pregnant, they must give birth before remarrying. While it is considered commendable to marry a widow, marriage to a widower or divorced man with children is less desirable for a woman's first marriage.

CHAPTER TEN

DIVORCE

T HE TENETS OF Islam make divorce a relatively straightforward affair. Islamic law does not require the parties to divulge the reason they seek a divorce. This eliminates the risk of perjury or family embarrassment. According to Muslim thinking, the public disclosure of unappeasable differences seldom motivates conciliation. On the contrary, it can estrange couples further. However, this does not mean that attempts are not made to settle disputes. Each party must appoint a mediator who tries to arrive at a mutually agreeable settlement. If these efforts fail, the divorce proceeds.

A man can dissolve his marriage by uttering the phrase "I divorce you". These words, not necessarily spoken in front of the spouse, must be reported to a *qadhi* in front of two witnesses in order for a formal document to be issued. For women, the process is not so easy. They must go to court to legalize the dissolution. Some Arab countries are making it easier for women to get out of a bad marriage but the trend has still not eroded Saudi Arabia's traditional bastions.

Despite its simplicity, the procedure is binding. The couple may remarry one another up to three times. After the third divorce, or if a spouse says "I divorce you thrice", the parties cannot remarry each other until the wife has married and divorced someone else first. Because of the severity of the action, such a drastic step is not usually taken without due consideration.

A divorce is not only void but forbidden unless the man is in a rational frame of mind and the woman is in a state of 'fresh purity'. This means it must be more than 40 days after childbirth or more than 10 days after her period. Nor can she have had intercourse after reaching this 'pure' state. When she enters a second state of 'fresh purity' a divorce may be decreed. This precaution determines whether or not the woman is pregnant. If she is not pregnant, she can remarry after a four-month waiting period called the 'iddah. If she is pregnant, the waiting period extends to the full term of the pregnancy, ensuring the child's legitimacy. During this time she remains the responsibility of her husband.

Women can have special rights included in their marriage contract. A qadhi can grant women a divorce for cause, including abuse, failure to support, and failure to maintain conjugal relations.

A man who initiates divorce proceedings has the obligation to support any children he has fathered by the divorced wife. A woman who divorces her husband may offer to return her dowry, depending on the conditions of the marriage contract.

Marriage contracts include provisions for divorce settlements. The usually high financial penalties provide another disincentive for divorce.

The divorced woman may return to her own family. This option offers emotional support during a transition period which may be fraught with stress. Children under the age of five usually remain with the mother. Beyond this age the father frequently claims full custody of male children. Girls normally stay with their mother.

Divorced women have the right to choose their own husbands. They usually remarry as a man's second wife.

CHAPTER ELEVEN

DEATH

USLIMS RECEIVE THE news of a death with the expression *Inna lillahi wa inna ilayhi rajiun* (we are of God and to God we shall return). In order not to prolong the anguish of the bereaved, Muslim burials take place as soon as possible after death. The body should be laid to rest before sunset on the day of the death but increasing bureaucracy often makes this impossible. Administrative procedure requires the identity of the deceased, the establishment of the next of kin, and a medical diagnosis of the cause of death before the body can be released for burial. Deaths caused by suspicious circumstances necessitate police intervention, inevitably resulting in further delays.

Upon issuance of the burial order, the body is washed, scented, and wrapped in white, unseamed cloth. A *surah* from the *Quran* is read before mourners go to the grave. Close male friends or family members carry the bier. Custom disallows women from accompanying the deceased to the grave in order to avoid emotional outbursts.

When a woman is buried, only her *mahram* (males whom she cannot marry) can uncover her face before lowering her body into the grave. The grave itself, which bears no headstone, is aligned in the direction of Makkah.

After burial, the three-day mourning period (*azza*) begins. Close male relatives go to the widow and other women of the family to announce the completion of the burial and to comfort the bereaved. During this time the bereaved family receives condolences and is generally cared for by the community. Saudi men and women always receive condolences separately.

The first day of an *azza* is the most emotionally draining. In cities particularly, it is more common for visitors to greet the bereaved and offer words of comfort and then join other guests seated in *majlis* fashion. Conversations are subdued.

Verses from the *Quran* are read and visitors remember the good qualities of the deceased. Because it is prohibited to make a ritual of mourning, overt displays of grief should cease after three days.

To ensure that she is not pregnant, a widow remains socially isolated for a period of four months and ten days. A divorcée remains isolated for three complete menstrual cycles. During this period of *'iddah* she receives no male visitors and minimizes attention to herself, including the wearing of jewellery and makeup.

If she is pregnant, her period of mourning extends to the time of childbirth. On the eve of the completion of mourning, the widow goes through a ritual cleansing, after which she may resume her normal activities.

A foreign woman who pays her condolences to a Saudi family should wear an *abaya* throughout the visit and refrain from wearing makeup, particularly lipstick.

Azzas are occasions of sadness, not business or social opportunities. The passing of business cards is not appropriate.

Islamic law clearly defines all possible permutations of inheritance. Outstanding debts and special bequests are paid from the deceased's estate before dividing the remainder among the heirs. In general, personal possessions of the deceased are not treasured as heirlooms but are disposed of.

CHAPTER TWELVE

ISLAM

N SAUDI ARABIA, Islam is not merely a religion but also a way of life. Its tenets guide all aspects of society, setting down codes of behaviour that include the most general and the most specific situations. Because Islam is an integral part of society in Saudi Arabia, non-Muslims living in the Kingdom should familiarize themselves with the basic concepts of the religion.

Islam means submission and, in Saudi Arabia particularly, this submission to God's will is absolute. The Western concept of state remaining separate from religion is alien to Islam.

The Muslim place of worship is called the mosque. In Saudi Arabia non-Muslims seldom enter mosques. Those who are invited should be particularly circumspect in both dress and behaviour. Shoes should be removed and left outside the entrance. The

interiors of mosques are devoid of furnishings or images depicting humans or animals. In accordance with Islam's teachings of equality, mosques have no places reserved for dignitaries.

Islam has no ordained clergy. Anyone may lead communal prayers but in the mosque it is usually an *imam* (religious figure) who performs this function and who delivers a sermon (*khutbah*) at the Friday noon prayer.

Makkah and Medina are Islam's holiest sites and only Muslims are allowed within the two cities' areas of sanctuary. Besides the fact that the Prophet Mohammed came from Makkah, the city has special prominence because it is here that the *Ka'ba* is located. Tradition holds that the Prophet Abraham and his son Ishmael laid its foundation. The building, situated in the centre courtyard of the Grand Mosque, is Islam's most sacred shrine.

The Quran

According to Islamic belief, the angel Gabriel began transmitting God's teachings to the Prophet Mohammed near Makkah in AD 610 for a period of 23 years. The *Quran* (meaning 'to recite' or 'to read aloud') documents these inspired revelations and is Islam's irrefutable source of reference.

The *surahs* (chapters) of the *Quran* were first committed to memory by Mohammed and his followers as they were received from God. Knowing that, over time, orally transmitted messages might be diluted or embellished, Mohammed instructed that the revelations should be written down according to his specific instructions concerning the arrangement of the verses and chapters. The resulting collation, the holy *Quran*, was completed in AD 651. Each of the 114 *surahs* comprises several verses (*ayas*). With the exception of the first chapter which is very short, chapters of the *Quran* are arranged in order of decreasing length, not in the order in which they were revealed. Some verses are in rhymes, others are prose. Combined, they represent the epitome of written Arabic. When read aloud, the power and beauty of the words can inspire great emotion in listeners.

The faithfully reproduced text has remained unchanged for more than 1,400 years. No variations are permitted. Muslims around the world study the *Quran* in Arabic because they believe that this is the only way to keep the message pure.

Further moral guidance comes from the *sunnah*. This is a collection of Prophet Mohammed's sayings and examples, each of which is referred to as a *hadith*.

The Five Pillars of Islam

A Muslim has five religious obligations, or *arkan* (pillars):

Shahada
The first pillar is *shahada*, or profession of faith: *Ashhadu an la ilaha illa-ilah, ashhadu an Mohammed rasool Allah* (I bear witness that there is no god but God; I bear witness that Mohammed is God's messenger). The recital of the *shahada* in full as an act of unquestioning and fervent belief is the sole requirement for conversion to Islam. The statement must be made aloud, understanding its significance, at least once in every Muslim's life.

Salaat

Prayers (*salaat*) performed in a prescribed manner comprise the second pillar of faith and are a foremost condition of Islam. Individually or in groups, in public or in private, Muslims ritually wash themselves, face in the direction of the *Ka'ba* in Makkah and pray five times daily: at dawn (*fajr*), midday (*dhuhr*), mid-afternoon (*asr*), sunset (*maghrib*), and nightfall (*isha*). In Saudi Arabia, all retail outlets are required to close for 20-30 minutes at each prayer time. Many businesses do not answer the telephone during prayer.

Zakaat

On a secular level, Islam requires its followers to care for the less fortunate. A compulsory philanthropy, called *zakaat* (almsgiving), is imposed on all Muslims. This duty is met through the payment of an annual religious tax at both the corporate and individual levels. *Zakaat* contributes to social stability and ensures that the needs of the community are not neglected.

Although it is not one of the five pillars of Islam, *kaffarah* is another charity-related requirement incorporated into the religion. *Kaffarah* serves as a form of penance whereby wrongdoers may absolve their sins by feeding the poor. Islam also encourages voluntary benevolence. *Sadaqa*, performed with a generosity of spirit, is philanthropy in the pure sense of the word. The needy receive particular attention at religious holidays when generous gifts of food and money are given.

Sawm

As the fourth pillar, fasting (*sawm*) is an act of worship. It not only serves as exacting self-discipline but teaches through experience the deprivations of thirst and hunger.

The daylight hours of Ramadan, the ninth month of the *hijira* calendar, are entirely devoted to this regimen. Exemptions are granted to pregnant, nursing, or menstruating women, the old or infirm, young children, the insane, and people travelling further than 80 kilometers. Anyone who breaks the fast must make up the days before the next Ramadan. Alternatively, they can feed one poor person for each fasting day missed.

Despite the difficulties of fasting, Muslims are expected to maintain their normal routines. Those who use Ramadan as an excuse to shirk work and other responsibilities effectively break their fast.

Although physical exertion noticeably diminishes during Ramadan, spiritual and social awareness increase. Muslims pray more, especially at night, spend more time studying the *Quran*, and perform more acts of charity. This unity of worship and sharing reinforces the spirit of brotherhood.

Besides physical abstention, Muslims must refrain from losing control of their temper and their speech. *One who does not give up speaking false words and acting by them is not required by God that he give up only his food and drink.*

Traditionally, the fast is broken after the sunset prayer with a light snack, often fresh dates and water. A more substantial meal is taken after the fifth prayer (*isha*), usually about 1 1/2 hours after dusk.

Hajj

Every Muslim shares the common religious goal of making the pilgrimage (*hajj*) to Makkah, the birthplace of the Prophet Mohammed and where he first received God's revelations. This fifth pillar of faith stipulates that the journey need be made only once in a lifetime and only if the pilgrim (*hajji*) is physically and financially able. *Hajj* cleanses pilgrims of sin; one prayer said in the Grand Mosque is equivalent to 100,000 prayers said elsewhere.

Islam preaches equality but perhaps nowhere is this more evident than during the pilgrimage. All pilgrims, regardless of social position, enter Makkah wearing a simple white seamless garment (*ihram*). Together, bound by their faith, they mingle to perform prescribed rituals of worship. Departure from the recognized pattern invalidates the pilgrimage.

As well as living their lives within the framework of the five pillars, Muslims have certain dietary restrictions: they may not consume intoxicating beverages, pork, blood, or animals which have not been slaughtered according to Islamic ritual. Foods which contain even minute percentages of forbidden ingredients are also forbidden. These include some gelatins and all products made with alcohol, such as pure vanilla extract.

Sects

Two main Muslim sects exist: the majority *Sunni*, or traditionalists, and the minority *Shia* (sometimes referred to as *Shiite*) whose name derives from the Arabic for 'partisans of Ali'. Although both branches share the same beliefs, they differ in political and structural orientation.

By example and strength of character, the Prophet Mohammed was able to unify his followers, regardless of their tribal loyalties. Ironically, it was the Prophet's death which caused discord and division, since he left no appointed successor. One faction, which became known as Sunni, believed that the *Khalipha* (successor) should be elected from the believers. Opposing Muslims, the *Shia*, maintained that Mohammed's cousin and son-in-law, Ali, should be his religious heir. The verbal conflict led to the AD 680 rebellion of Ali's followers against the ruling Caliph and resulted in a massacre of the attackers.

CHAPTER THIRTEEN

THE LAW

I F FOREIGNERS FIND Saudi customs unfamiliar, they find the machinations of local law even more confusing. Expatriates tend to get themselves into trouble through ignorance or misunderstanding rather than deliberate transgression. The end result, however, is the same for everyone: sanctioned retribution.

Sharia

Sharia ('the path') is the legal framework of Islam. It attempts to strike a workable balance between mercy and the solution to social problems. Yet to people whose only

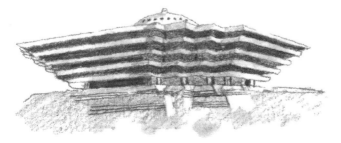

contact with it is the dramatically recounted punishments presented in the media, the system is at once fascinating and fearful. Few non-Muslims know more about *Sharia* than the much quoted *an eye for an eye, a tooth for a tooth.*

Sharia derives primarily from two sources: the *Quran*, Islam's holy book comprising God's revelations to the Prophet Mohammed, and the *sunnah*, examples of Mohammed's deeds and approvals concerning social matters. Lesser sources are *ijma*, a consensus of religious scholars, and *qiya*, which calls on interpretation based on precedence. Situations not covered in the *Quran* are called 'regulations', such as Labour Regulations.

Sharia is not secular, but ethical. Crimes are thus committed against the will of God—an unthinkable act. This, more than the harsh punishments, explains the Kingdom's low crime rate.

Saudi Arabia follows the Hanbali school of law. It strongly emphasizes the four acknowledged sources of reference and does not allow liberal influences.

As an integral part of Islam, *Sharia* embraces all aspects of communal and individual behaviour. In protecting the social order, *Sharia* places the rights of society over the rights of individuals, who are viewed as parts of the whole. Those who violate the peace and security of the community risk punishment proportional to the magnitude of the crime.

Procedure

Although the code seems alien and harsh to the uninformed, in fact it has much in common with most systems practised in the West. The accused remains innocent until proven guilty or until he offers a confession of guilt. The onus of proof rests with the accuser who must provide a minimum of two eyewitnesses to the crime. Alternatively, the accuser may demand an oath of innocence from the defendant.

In both civil and criminal proceedings a *qadhi* acts as judge and jury. The defendant has the right to appeal the *qadhi's* decision. *Sharia* does not recognise precedence. Each legal decision is independent of all others and is not binding on any future decisions. Legal costs are not recoverable. Awarded damages reflect actual costs. There is no compensation for such intangibles as emotional distress or lost opportunity. Non-religious courts are referred to as 'committees'. The Labour Court hears disputes in employer/employee relations.

Interrogations are carried out in Arabic. Translators are provided when necessary. The suspect should not sign his statement until he is convinced that the Arabic text correctly records his account of the events.

Punishments

Sentencing usually takes place without undue delay. Prison terms include the time served before the trial. It is wise to remember that imprisonment is not only the result of conviction but may occur during investigations and until settlement of seemingly minor disputes.

Death sentences are carried out swiftly. In the case of murder, punishment may be determined by the victim's family rather than by the court. Sometimes the convicted person must wait for the victim's children to come of age and decide whether they want the accused to die or whether they will accept blood money in compensation.

Murderers and rapists suffer public decapitation; adulterers face death by stoning. Repeated theft is punishable by amputation of the right hand, although thieves who steal out of hunger or real need are let go; only crimes of greed are punishable. For these more serious offenses, the sentence must pass the high courts and receive final approval of the King before being carried out. Less severe penalties include public floggings, jail terms, fines, and deportation for non-Saudis. A flogging is intended to be more injurious to the pride than to the body.

Common Pitfalls

Many of the foreigners who spend time in Saudi jails are there for activities which are legal in their own countries but illegal here. The most common pitfalls concern offenses related to traffic, alcohol, business, and morality.

Despite the apparent lack of blame of one of the parties, culpability in traffic accidents is apportioned on a percentage basis. Even the apparently blameless party may end up sharing some of the responsibility.

The consumption, brewing, purchase, or sale of alcohol is illegal in the Kingdom. Foreigners who choose to ignore the law are particularly at risk if they compound the act by supplying alcohol to Saudis.

Restrictions on the public interaction of men and women cause another significant hazard, particularly for single-status foreigners. Unmarried couples who socialize publicly, such as eating in restaurants or shopping together, are in contravention of local moral laws and may be jailed or, in extreme cases, deported.

The guardians of moral standards arc called *mutawwa*. They oversee virtue according to their own specific interpretations of Islam and enforce it vigorously. Offences vary from wearing overly vivid lipstick to travelling as unrelated man and woman together in a car. The *mutawwa* can be identified by their large beards and short *thobes*.

The Saudi government states that no arrests or even approaches by the *mutawwa* can be made unless a civic policeman is in attendance. If approached by a *mutawwa*, whether he is alone or accompanied by a policeman, handle the situation politely for as long as possible, trying to diffuse the situation. It is better to acquiesce than to risk turning the situation into irreversible open hostility.

Because of discrepancies in what is considered acceptable and unacceptable, foreigners are well advised not only to become conversant with basic regulations which might affect their business and personal lives, but also to obey the law of the land or to accept the consequences.

Visas and Other Documents

The intensely private nature of Saudi society translates into a hesitancy to open the country to strangers whose traditions are often in conflict with the conservative habits of the local population. Restrictions are easing but travel to the Kingdom is still relatively controlled. The following are descriptions of the various visas issued by the Kingdom:

Residence Visas

Obtaining a residence visa to Saudi Arabia usually takes much time, patience, and paperwork. Allow six weeks for the process. In addition to providing the employment contract, academic records, marriage certificate (if the applicant is bringing his family), and professional qualifications, applicants must undergo a medical examination that includes an AIDS test.

Business/Visit Visas

A letter of invitation that includes a visa number is sent by a corporate or individual sponsor to the visitor's country of residence. This letter and the applicant's passport must be delivered to the local Saudi Embassy. Without the vital visa number, no visa will be issued. Visas are valid only for one *hijira* month (see chapter 15) from the date of issue.

Business or Visit visas are not necesarily granted as a matter of course. The procedure has been simplified for many nationalities but sporadic complications continue to arise. Foreign women, especially unmarried women, travelling on their own are regarded with suspicion. This is because Saudi women traditionally do not travel without an accompanying male family member—one whom they either cannot marry or to whom they are already married. Overcoming such cultural obstacles can be challenging for women with business in Saudi Arabia or for those who would like to visit their families.

Exit/Re-entry or Exit Only Visas

Depending on circumstances, one of these visas is required by residents who wish to leave the Kingdom. The *iqama* (residence document) must be surrendered once the visa has been acquired. The procedure generally takes at least two days although emergency visas can be obtained in a few hours. To be on the safe side, make visa applications one or two weeks before the departure date. Allow even more time prior to the major '*eid* holidays. It is advisable to keep a stock of passport pictures for visa applications. Once a visa has been issued, it must be used or be officially cancelled before the expiration date. Failure to comply with this regulation results in a fine of SR1,000.

Tourist Visas

Saudi Arabia now issues tourist visas in restricted numbers to restricted categories of candidates. The visas are obtained as part of a tour package with government-appointed travel agents. Consult Saudi Arabian Airlines for a list of agents.

Hajj/Umrah Visas

Muslims wishing to perform *hajj* or *umrah* must apply for the applicable visa in their country of residence. Quotas are enforced. In the case of converts or applicants who don't have Muslim names, documentary evidence will be required to prove the applicant is a Muslim.

With the exception of citizens of other Gulf countries, all foreigners coming to the Kingdom must have a Saudi sponsor. This is an individual or company who is responsible for them during their stay. Hotels in Saudi Arabia are not permitted to sponsor visitors. Visa extensions are obtainable only through the visitor's sponsor. It is important to note that visas are issued according to the *hijira* calendar. The *hijira* year is 11 days *shorter* than the Gregorian year. A visitor who thinks he can stay for a month according to the Gregorian calendar system will run into difficulties when he tries to leave the Kingdom unless he has asked his sponsor to grant a visa extension.

Visas will not be put into passports that are due to expire within six months. An Israeli stamp in the passport can also cause problems.

Visitors should carry their passports with them. Legally employed residents must carry an identity document called an *iqama*. This is issued after receipt of the residence visa. Dependents can either carry their passports or a photocopy of the employee's *iqama* which lists accompanying family members. New regulations allow highly qualified professionals (doctors, engineers, etc.) to keep their passports in their possession. Other employees must surrender their passports to their employers.

Immigration and Customs

Customs restrictions are relatively few: alcohol, pork products, pornography, firearms, and drugs. Unofficially, non-Islamic religious articles are also included. The scope of interpretation about what comprises these categories, however, can be broad indeed. Certain diet pills which may have banned substances, for example, can land the importer in jail. Fashion magazines may be confiscated or have offending pages—models with bare arms or legs—

torn out. Videos and computer diskettes are liable to be checked for inappropriate content. Christmas trees and ornaments, while not religious in nature, are associated with a religious celebration and are as such technically unacceptable.

Baggage searches are usually thorough and not always orderly. Businessmen bringing in special equipment or presentation materials may choose to have a representative of their Saudi sponsor help them clear Customs.

Anyone anticipating a move to the Kingdom is advised to check with a Saudi embassy or consulate or with other expats who are already familiar with the system in order to avoid the distress of having seemingly innocent belongings confiscated.

Driving Licenses

Saudi Arabia is the only country in the world where women are forbidden by law to drive. Instead they rely on male family members, hired drivers, or taxis to get them to and from their destinations.

Despite the staggering number of lost work hours as men transport children from school and take their women on errands and to appointments, and, alternatively, the expense of hiring chauffers, the system prevails. Religious conservatives argue that it would be unacceptable if a woman driving alone had a breakdown or was in an accident and required the help of non-family males.

Foreign men who take up residency in the Kingdom simply have to present a valid driving license to the licensing authority. They will then be issued with a Saudi driving license. Visitors can rent cars using their current license.

CHAPTER FOURTEEN

GOVERNMENT

HE KINGDOM OF Saudi Arabia officially came into being in 1932 as a result of the successful efforts of the charismatic leader, Abdul Aziz, to unify tribes and territory throughout much of Arabia. The Kingdom's name derives from the tribal name of Abdul Aziz, 'Al-Saud'.

Although Saudi Arabia is ruled by a king, the country is not a monarchy in the Western sense. Unlike other hereditary systems of government, succession in Saudi Arabia is not based on primogeniture; instead, senior members of the Al-Saud family consult with each other and decide which of them is best suited to be Crown Prince and then King. All the kings to date have been sons of Abdul Aziz.

The official government emblem is the palm tree over crossed swords. The palm symbolizes vitality, growth, and prosperity, while the swords represent strength and justice. This emblem is also used by members of the

Royal Family, whether or not they hold government positions.

Saudi Arabia's distinctive green flag has the Arabic text *There is no God but Allah, and Mohammed is His messenger* inscribed over a single horizontal sword. The flag does not fly at half mast during periods of mourning.

System of Government

The Saudi method of ruling is a synthesis of traditional values which includes, first and foremost, a commitment to the teachings of Islam followed by lineage and strong leadership. It is the duty of the King, as both religious and secular leader, to ensure an ongoing compatibility between faith and government. In a region which has a history of political volatility, the leadership of the Al-Saud family has been a record of unbroken peace and stability. This can be attributed to a system of government which, overall, responds to the needs of the people.

The King also carries the titles of Prime Minister and Commander-in-Chief of the Armed Forces. King Fahd added the title Custodian of the Two Holy Mosques. The King appoints the Crown Prince who serves as First Deputy Prime Minister.

The Majlis

The *majlis*, an assembly of young and old male relatives and friends, is a classic Arab tradition and Saudi Arabia's most basic form of government. The practice cuts across class and sectarian lines and preserves social cohesion. Ordinary citizens may petition the King and other officials directly and expect that appropriate action will be taken.

The Royal Diwan

The King's executive office, his private office, and the offices of his principal advisers and heads of several government departments are located in the Royal Diwan. Here the routine business of running the country is conducted. Here, too, the King holds his regular *majlis* where he receives petitions from his subjects.

The Council of Ministers

In 1953, the Council of Ministers was formed as one way to cope with the problems of rapid modernization as well as tribal and regional differences. This represented the first step towards a national administrative system.

The Council exercises both legislative and executive powers and is headed by the King, followed by the First Deputy Prime Minister (the Crown Prince). In addition to the heads of each of the 21 ministries, the council comprises ministers without portfolio and specially appointed advisors. Cabinet ministers serve a four-year term. The King can grant four-year extensions by Royal Decree.

The Council of Ministers carries out the active business of government. Only resolutions passed by a majority vote are binding. In the event of a tie, the King casts the deciding ballot. The King must approve all Council decisions before they can be implemented.

Consultative Council

This traditional method of governing was restructured by King Fahd in 1992 and inaugurated in 1993. Known in Arabic as the *majlis as-shoura*, the Consultative Council's primary purpose is to advise the King on matters of policy and planning. The several groups within the framework of the Council sit regularly to study questions relating to politics, economics, education and other national concerns. The Council works indirectly with the Cabinet to issue laws.

The Council President and 60 members are selected for a four-year period by the King from a cross-section of citizens throughout the country. The combined talents of businessmen, educators, former government officials, and other professionals ensure a balanced input. Each member must be well qualified, have a good reputation, and be a Saudi national, not just by birth but also by origin.

Provincial Government

Saudi Arabia is divided into 13 provinces, each of which is administered by a Governor (*Amir*) and regional officers. Local advisory councils appointed by the King and headed by the Governor and his executives consist of at least 10 private citizens with special areas of expertise. There is a total of 20 members who sit on each council. Various subcommittees concentrate on specific issues relating to the province. Reports from provincial councils go to the Ministry of Interior which then passes them to appropriate agencies for action.

SAUDI ARABIA'S PROVINCES AND THEIR CAPITALS

Riyadh Province:	**Riyadh**
Makkah Province:	**Makkah**
Madinah Province:	**Madinah**
Al-Qasim Province:	**Buraidah**
Eastern Province:	**Dammam**
Asir Province:	**Abha**
Tabuk Province:	**Tabuk**
Hail Province:	**Hail**
Northern Border Province:	**Ar'ar**
Jizan Province:	**Jizan**
Najran Province:	**Najran**
Al-Baha Province:	**Al-Baha**
Al-Jouf Province:	**Sakakah**

GOVERNMENT DEPARTMENTS

National Guard
Ministry of Defense and Aviation
Ministry of Interior
Ministry of Foreign Affairs
Ministry of Petroleum and Mineral Resources
Ministry of Finance and National Economy
Ministry of Municipalities and Rural Affairs
Ministry of Housing and Public Works
Ministry of Higher Education
Ministry of Education
Presidency of Women's Education
Ministry of Hajj
Ministry of Islamic Affairs
Ministry of Labour and Social Affairs
Ministry of Communications
Ministry of Justice
Ministry of Information
Ministry of Posts, Telegraphs, and Telephones
Ministry of Industry and Electricity
Ministry of Commerce
Ministry of Health
Ministry of Agriculture
Ministry of Planning
Presidency of Youth Welfare

CHAPTER FIFTEEN

THE MUSLIM YEAR

OST SAUDIS REFER primarily to the lunar or *hijira* calendar. Unlike the Gregorian calendar, which is based on the rotation of the earth around the sun, the lunar calendar follows the movements of the moon. While astronomers and mathematicians can make accurate calculations as to when each month will begin, the *Quran* requires an actual sighting (*ru'iya*) of the new moon to mark the official start of a month. This becomes particularly significant when announcing the commencement of fasting for the holy month of Ramadan.

The lunar calendar has 12 months of 28 to 30 days, or 354 days per year. Depending on the sightings of the new moons, the lunar year is generally 11 days shorter than the 365-day solar year. It is rare for Ramadan to occur twice in the same year. This rotation enables all Muslims to experience the discipline of

Ramadan in every season. Every 32 1/2 years particular dates will coincide, for example 1 January/1 *Muharram* (the first month of the *hijira* calendar). Unlike other lunar calendars, the Islamic one does not add a thirteenth month. The *hijira* months therefore do not keep in line with the seasons.

The Muslim calendar was begun by Caliph Omar. It takes its starting point from 16 June AD 622, the year of the *hijira* (emigration) of the Prophet Muhammad and his followers from Makkah to Medina to escape persecution. Thus, the year AD 2002 corresponds to 1422/1423 H (*hijira*). The longer solar year accounts for the slight discrepancy in the difference between the first *hijira* year and the current Gregorian year.

Because the term 'AD' (*Anno Domini*) conflicts with Muslim beliefs, Gregorian years are often referred to as 'CE' (Christian Era) and sometimes as 'G', i.e. 2002 G.

Saudis also follow a solar astrological calendar. This corresponds to the Gregorian calendar but months are referred to by their zodiac names. The national budget and school holidays follow the zodiac calendar.

The 12 Muslim months are: *Muharram, Safar, Rabi' I (Rabi' al-Awwal), Rabi' II (Rabi' ath-Thani), Jumadi I (Jumadi al-Ula), Jumadi II (Jumadi al-Akhirah), Rajab, Sha'ban, Ramadan, Shawwal, Dhu al-Qida, and Dhu al-Hijah.*

Friday is the weekly day of rest, although government offices and many companies in the private sector also close on Thursday afternoon or all day. The special Friday noon prayer at the mosque is particularly well attended.

Holidays and Holy Days

Ramadan
The ninth month of the Muslim calendar is considered to be especially holy. It was during Ramadan that God first began his revelations to the Prophet Mohammed. These revelations continued for 23 years. Between dawn and dusk throughout Ramadan, Muslims abstain from food, drink, and sensual pleasures, and devote themselves to more spiritual endeavours. The first light of dawn is generally accepted to occur when a white thread can be distinguished from a black one, approximately two hours before sunrise.

In deference to people who are fasting, non-Muslims should refrain from eating, drinking, or smoking in public during the day throughout the month of Ramadan. Dress and behaviour should be particularly circumspect during this period.

Lailat al-Qadr (Night of Power and Greatness)
This takes place on one of the odd-numbered nights of the last 10 days of Ramadan, subject to lunar sightings – often the 27th of Ramadan. It is characterised by increased spiritual activity and commemorates the occasion of Mohammed receiving his first revelations. The faithful believe that prayers of petition made on this night will be answered.

Shawwal I—Eid al-Fitr
This 'lesser feast', is a period of special celebration and festivity. It serves as a transition from the strict abstinence of Ramadan to the normal routine of the rest of the year. The holiday usually continues to the second or third day of the month of *Shawwal*, though government offices and some businesses close for longer.

After communal prayers, usually at dawn, families and friends gather to feast. During the day they exchange visits and gifts. The celebration is marked by wearing new clothes and eating distinctive *'eid* sweets. Just as Ramadan is a time of spiritual bonding, the *'eid* reinforces social ties and encourages generosity.

Dhu al-Hijah 9–12

The Fifth Pillar of Islam requires Muslims to make a pilgrimage (*hajj*) to Makkah at least once in their lifetime if they are physically and financially able. This duty must be performed during the specified days and according to specified rituals.

Dhu al-Hijah 10—Eid al-Adha

This feast of sacrifice, or 'greater feast', signifies the end of the *hajj*. Animals are slaughtered in commemoration of Abraham's willingness to sacrifice his son. Much of the meat is distributed to the poor. As with *'Eid al-Fitr*, Muslims offer special prayers, dress in new clothes, visit each other, and offer gifts, particularly to children. Business and government offices close during these festivities which last from four days to two weeks, depending on whether the organization is government or non-government.

Saudi National Day

On this day in 1932, King Abdul Aziz formally founded the Kingdom of Saudi Arabia. Saudis celebrate the occasion on the first of *Meezan* (first of Libra) which is equivalent to 23 September. This is the only official celebration which falls on the same date each year in the Gregorian calendar.

CHAPTER SIXTEEN
DOs AND DON'Ts

VERY CULTURE HAS its code of conduct. Foreigners in Saudi Arabia often find adaptation difficult simply because they assume that the customs of such an alien society will be incompatible with their own recognized values.

Ignorance of what Saudis deem right and wrong breeds insecurity; insecurity inhibits relaxed cultural interaction. Expatriates who benefit most from their stay in Saudi Arabia have made an effort to understand and follow the Kingdom's precepts of acceptable behaviour. They find that the rules are generally logical, reasonable, and often surprisingly similar to familiar social standards.

The following quick reference encapsulates the various dos and don'ts already mentioned. This list is arranged according to the related chapters where more detailed information on each subject can be found.

Chapter 1 — Hospitality

❖ Do not use ritual expressions such as "Let's get together for lunch" unless you mean what you say or you risk compromising your sincerity in the eyes of Arab friends or colleagues.

❖ Enquire about the individual and his or her family but, unless a friendship has already been formed, men should not ask about other men's wives, nor should women ask about other women's husbands.

❖ Do not discuss unpleasant topics in social situations.

❖ Be flexible about punctuality when inviting Arab guests and don't arrive too early at large Saudi functions.

❖ Greet/serve the eldest person first, regardless of his or her social status.

❖ Accept the first cup of coffee as an acknowledgement of the host's hospitality, even if you choose not to drink it.

❖ Do not accept more than three cups of coffee unless socializing with close friends.

❖ Gently wobble the coffee cup from side to side or cover it with the palm of the hand to indicate that nothing more is required. Return the cup with the right hand.

❖ Politely refuse a spontaneous invitation once or twice before accepting graciously.

❖ If possible, reply to a written invitation in the same language in which it is received.

❖ Arrive punctually when invited by a Saudi.

❖ Do not assume that an invitation to a Saudi social function includes men and women. Even if both are invited, it is likely that the sexes will be segregated.

❖ When inviting more than one Saudi to a private gathering, discreetly ensure that each feels comfortable with the other(s) in a purely social situation.

❖ Try to comply with local custom when eating with traditional Saudi families.

❖ Do not let the fingers touch the mouth or tongue when eating from a communal dish.

❖ Accept offerings of food from other Saudi guests; remember to reciprocate. Handle food with the first three fingers only.

❖ Leave a portion of the meal uneaten.

❖ Depart after the presentation of incense or soon after the meal has finished.

Chapter 4 — Dress

❖ Do not ask a Saudi gentleman to remove his head covering.

❖ Do not expect a Saudi woman to unveil in front of men who are not members of her family.

❖ Dress circumspectly in public.

Chapter 5 — Social Convention

❖ Call a Saudi by his/her given name. This can be proceeded by Mr./Mrs./Ms. until a more familiar relationship develops.

❖ Address members of the Royal Family as Your Royal Highness/Your Highness or Prince/Princess (name), even if they introduce themselves without reference to their title.

❖ Do not prematurely withdraw if a Saudi gentleman holds your hand.

❖ Men and women should avoid physical contact in public.

❖ Try to resolve problems without conflict and allow Saudis to extricate themselves from awkward situations without losing face.

❖ Do not risk a relationship by pushing for satisfactory outcomes to commitments which exceed capabilities.

❖ A man should not give a gift to a Saudi for his wife unless they are family friends.

❖ Be careful that business gifts are not misinterpreted as bribery.

❖ Do not show too much admiration for a Saudi's possessions in case he feels obliged to offer the item under discussion.

❖ Do not expose the soles of the feet to Saudis or make idiomatic references to shoes.

❖ Do not beckon or point with the finger.

❖ Make a dedicated effort to learn at least basic courteous phrases in Arabic.

❖ Exercise caution when photographing certain scenery or architecture. The motives may be misinterpreted.

❖ Do not photograph people, particularly women, without first asking permission.

❖ Do not photograph military installations or government structures without prior approval.

Chapter 6 — Striking a Bargain

❖ Always offer ritual greetings and enter into social dialogue before beginning bargaining or business discussions.

❖ Do not become impatient if negotiations seem to drag on.

❖ Know the value of the item being negotiated.

❖ Be prepared to bargain. Sometimes the tactic also works in fixed-price stores.

❖ Learn to enjoy the experience of bargaining. It should not become a contest of wills.

❖ Do not let the theatrics of bargaining intimidate you into making unnecessary concessions.

❖ Recognize when negotiations are at a dead end.

Chapter 7 — Doing Business

❖ Allow extra time allotments in business schedules for unexpected or rescheduled meetings.

❖ Do not react to the expression *Insha'allah* with cynicism.

❖ Try not to arrive unannounced at a Saudi office.

❖ Be prepared to devote time and energy towards building and sustaining new relationships.

❖ Be discerning in the disclosure of information.

❖ Do not criticize a Saudi directly, particularly in front of others. Highlight positive points first.

❖ Do not rush into the discussion of business. The preliminary period of social conversation can be used to learn potentially useful information.

❖ Do not push Saudis into making a business decision. Numerous factors may be influencing their hesitancy to commit, not least of which is the desire not to cause offense by saying 'no'.

❖ Print business cards in English on one side and Arabic on the other. As a courtesy, translate presentation documents into Arabic but make sure the translation is checked by a reliable, qualified person.

❖ Be accommodating and compromise when necessary.

❖ Walk a Saudi visitor to the door/elevator to show respect.

Chapter 11 — Death

❖ Women should wear an *abaya* and not wear makeup when attending a Saudi *azza*.

❖ Do not hand out business cards at a funeral or *azza*.

Chapter 12 — Islam

❖ Become familiar with the basic concepts of Islam.

❖ Do not enter mosques in Saudi Arabia unless specifically invited by a Saudi friend, in which case leave your shoes outside the entrance.

Chapter 13 — The Law

❖ Do not sign statements written in Arabic unless convinced that the text correctly records your account of the alleged infraction.

❖ Become conversant with regulations which might affect your business and personal life.

❖ Allow plenty of time for visa applications. Make sure your passport is valid for at least six months and that it has no Israeli stamps in it. Remember that the period of visa validity relates to the shorter *hijira* calendar.

❖ Always carry an identity document, either a passport or *iqama* or a photocopy of either of these documents if the original is not available.

❖   In order to avoid problems with Customs officials, check with Saudi authorities or other expat residents concerning restricted items.

Chapter 15 — The Muslim Year

❖   Be particularly circumspect in dress and behaviour during the holy month of Ramadan.

❖   Do not eat, drink, or smoke in public during daylight hours in Ramadan.

GLOSSARY

abaya	black, full-length outer garment worn by Saudi women
abu	father
Amir	governor, prince, or tribal leader
arkan	pillars, as in 'Five Pillars of Faith'
asr	mid-afternoon; the third of five daily prayers
athl	tamarisk, a wood used in the local manufacture of incense burners
aya	verse (from the *Quran*)
azza	three-day mourning period
baksheesh	complimentary 'extra' given after negotiations have been completed. Although foreigners use the term positively, in reality the word has negative connotations of bribery
bin	son of; descriptor following a given male name and preceding a father's, grandfather's, or great-grandfather's name

bint	daughter of; descriptor following a female given name and preceding a father's, grandfather's, or great-grandfather's name
bisht	full-length, lightweight cloak of beige, brown or black wool worn by Saudi men. Also called a *mishlah*
burqa	face mask which has eye openings, worn by women in some areas of Saudi Arabia
dallah	pelican-beaked coffee pot
dehn al ward	extract of crushed rose petals
dhun al-faghiya	oil concentrate from the henna flower
Dhu al-Qida	eleventh month of the *hijira* calendar
Dhu al-Hijah	twelfth month of the *hijira* calendar
dhuhr	midday; the second of five daily prayers
digla	elegant, full-length tailored coat
djambiya	a dagger encased in a sharply curved sheath covered with leather or ornately decorated silver
'eid	holiday
'Eid Al-Adha	period of sacrificial offerings and festivities at the end of the *hajj* (pilgrimage)
'Eid al-Fitr	period of special celebration and festivity after Ramadan
ethmid	a now rare stone which consists mainly of antimony trisulphide, an inert substance ideal for *kohl*
fajr	dawn; the first of five daily prayers
faghiya	henna flower
farwa	long coat lined with sheepskin worn by Saudi men in cold weather

ghutrah	white head covering worn by Saudi men
hadith	traditions and sayings of Prophet Mohammed
hail	cardamom
hajj	pilgrimage
hajji	pilgrim
helba	a foul-tasting seed that can be boiled in water or taken as a powder. It is an effective remedy for bone injuries
hijira	flight of the Prophet Mohammed from Makkah to Medina
hinna'	henna, a rich dye frequently used in the Middle East
hubbly-bubbly	see *shisha*
ibn	son of; descriptor following a given male name and preceding the father's, grandfather's, and great-grandfather's name
'iddah	period of four months and 10 days which a divorced woman must wait before she can remarry
igaal	black, braided chord which rests on the *ghutrah* or *yashmakh*
ijma	a consensus of religious scholars, particularly concerning matters pertaining to *Sharia* law
Insha'allah	'If it is God's will', a frequently used expression
iqama	identity document required to be carried by all expatriate employees at all times

ihram	seamless white cotton garment worn by pilgrims
imam	person who leads communal prayers and delivers Friday sermons
isha	fifth of five daily prayers
Jumadi I (Jumadi al-Ula)	fifth month of the *hijira* calendar
Jumadi II (Jumadi al-Akhirah)	sixth month of the *hijira* calendar
ka'ba	Islam's holiest shrine, the foundation of which was laid by Abraham
kaffarah	a charity-related requirement incorporated into Islam whereby a wrongdoer may absolve sins by feeding the poor
karkaday	dried hibiscus flowers. The infusion can be served hot or cold. It reputedly fights colds and stabilized blood pressure
Khalifa	successor; 'caliph' in English
khutbah	sermon delivered at noon prayer on Fridays
kohl	a black powder usually made from antimony trisulphide or lead sulphide. In Arabic, *kohl* refers to any substance that goes on the eyelid or the margin of the eye
laban	a yoghurt drink, formerly made from camel's milk but now commonly produced from cow's milk
lailat al-hinna'	'night of henna'; the night before a wedding

lailat al-Qadr	night of power and greatness (Ramadan 27)
leefah	dried palm webbing placed in the spout of a traditional coffee pot (*dallah*) for filtration
ma'amoul	round, dark balls of incense. The ingredients can include powdered *'ood* and concentrates of amber, musk, saffron, and oil of *'ood*
maghrib	sunset; the fourth of five daily prayers
mahmasa	long-handled, ladle-like cooking utensil
mahr	dowry
mahram	males whom a Muslim woman cannot marry
majlis	a gathering; the tradition of easy, informal accessibility to leaders
majlis as-shoura	Consultative Council comprising a president and 60 members selected for a four-year period by the King from a cross-section of citizens
Meezan	ninth month of the Saudi solar (zodiac) calendar, equivalent to Libra portion of the Gregorian calendar
medkhana	incense burner or censer
milkah	premarital contract
mishlah	traditional, full-length, lightweight cloak of brown or black wool worn by Saudi men. Also called a *bisht*
miswak	predecessor of the toothbrush. The slightly bitter-tasting stick comes from the root of the arak tree

mu'zzin	person whose intonations call the faithful to prayer
mubarrad	wooden coffee box or tray
mubkhara	traditional incense burner or censer
Muharram	first month of the *hijira* calendar
murrah	meaning 'bitter', an incense of great value referred to in English as myrrh
mutawwa	member of the Society for Virtue and the Prevention of Vice, commonly referred to as religious police
muwahhidun	unitarians; the term by which the followers of the religious reformer Mohammed Abdul-Wahhab are correctly referred
na'al	traditional leather sandals
nanaa	a hot infusion made with fresh mint
narghile	See *shisha*
nijr	mortar
om	mother
'ood	collective term for scented woods
qadhi	judge
qahwa	coffee
qiya	interpretations based on previous similar situations
Quran	Islam's holy book conveying the word of God
Rabi' I (Rabi' al-Awwal)	third month of the *hijira* calendar
Rabi' II (Rabi' a-Thani)	fourth month of the *hijira* calendar
Rajab	seventh month of the *hijira* calendar

Ramadan	ninth month of the *hijira* calendar
ru'iya	sighting of the new moon
rutab	the third stage of a date's development, when the fruit is half brown and half yellow or red. The first stage is *khalal*, which produces green, bitter tasting fruit; the second stage is *balah*, when the fruit is at the red or yellow stage and most nutritious, and the fourth stage is *tamr*, the 'cooked' stage when the date is fully ripened and completely brown.
sadaqa	voluntary benevolence, particularly in evidence at religious holidays
Safar	second month of the *hijira* calendar
salah	prayer (*pl. salaat*); second pillar of Islam
sawm	fasting; fourth pillar of Islam
Sha'ban	eighth month of the *hijira* calendar
shahada	profession of faith; first pillar of Islam
sham'agh	the red-and-white head covering worn by Saudi men (also referred to as *yashmakh*)
Sharia	Islamic law
sheikh	a title given to a tribal leader or to a man who has earned stature in the community through age, wealth, or influence
Shawwal	tenth month of the *hijira* calendar
Shia	one of two main Muslim sects. The name derives from the Arabic for "partisans of Ali"
Shiite	Muslim religious sect, sometimes referred to as *Shia*

shisha	a tall elegant smoking aparatus consisting of a water-filled base, a rigid and flexible tube, and a clay bowl which holds the tobacco mixture (also called *narghile)*
sirwaal	long, white drawstring pantaloons worn under a *thobe*
subhah	a special gift of gold or jewellery given by the groom to the bride on the morning after their marriage has been consummated
sufra	a circular mat woven from palm fronds or other similar material on which dishes of food are placed
sunnah	accounts of Prophet Mohammed's sayings and examples
Sunni	one of the two main Muslim sects. The word means 'traditionalists'
surah	verse from the *Quran*
suq	market place. For example, the carpet *suq* specialises in the sale of carpets, vegetables are bought at the vegetable *suq*, etc
Tal Omrek	a form of address which shows particular respect
taqiyah	white skull cap worn by Saudi men to keep the *ghutrah* or *shamagh* in place
taher	ritual purification

tamr	see *rutab*
tarha	black gauze scarf worn by Saudi women to cover their hair
thobe	full-length, long-sleeved, shirt-like garb worn by Saudi men
umrah	the 'lesser' pilgrimage performed on an individual basis at times other than *hajj*
wagiya	denomination of weight equivalent to one troy ounce (31.1 grams)
wudho'a	ritual cleansing, particularly required before prayer
yad al-mahmasa	a long-handled implement with a broad, flat end, used to stir roasting coffee beans
yansoon	aniseed; a hot infusion used to soothe coughs and treat indigestion, flatulence and colic
yashmakh	red-and-white checked head covering worn by Saudi men
zaghareet	shrill sound made by the rapid vibration of the tongue against the back of the upper teeth while holding a high-pitched note
zakaat	obligatory almsgiving; third pillar of Islam
zhooraat	a blend of flower petals

OTHER BOOKS BY KATHY CUDDIHY:

An A to Z of Places and Things Saudi
Motherhood: Marriage's Occupational Hazard
Familiarity Breeds Content
The Hostess Book
Gifts of Arabia